Single Parents by Choice

A Growing Trend in Family Life

Single Parents by Choice

A Growing Trend in Family Life

Naomi Miller, Ph.D.

INSIGHT BOOKS

Plenum Press · New York and London

HQ
759.915
M55
1992
X

Library of Congress Cataloging-in-Publication Data

Miller, Naomi.
   Single parents by choice ; a growing trend in family life / Naomi
Miller.
      p.   cm.
   Includes bibliographical references (p.   ) and index.
   ISBN 0-306-44321-X
   1. Single parents. 2. Single mothers. 3. Single-parent family.
I. Title.
HQ759.915.M55 1992
306.85'6--dc20   92-17494
                                                            CIP

ISBN 0-306-44321-X

© 1992 Plenum Press, New York
A Division of Plenum Publishing Corporation
233 Spring Street, New York, N.Y. 10013

An Insight Book

Printed in the United States of America

96932

For Alan
and our children

Acknowledgments

I would like to express my deep thanks to the many people who so graciously agreed to be interviewed by me and to share their experience of parenting, as well as many other personal details of their lives. Without their willingness to discuss their struggles, frustrations, and joys in an open and forthright fashion, this book could not have come about.

I am especially grateful to the following people who agreed to read selected portions of my manuscript and share their comments with me: David Blankenhorn; the Honorable Gertrud T. Mainzer; Paula L. Ettelbrick, Esq.; George Getzel, D.S.W.; Sondra Farganis, Ph.D.; Blanche Gelber, Esq.; and Jane Mattes, Ph.D. I would also like to thank the numerous people I interviewed in various fields of expertise who so freely gave both of their time and their interest. I would especially like to thank the staff at the National Center for Health Statistics in Washington, DC for their patience and perseverance in helping me both to understand and to locate relevant statistical data.

My grateful thanks to Norma Fox, Executive Editor of Insight Books, for having faith in me, and last, but not least, to my husband, Alan W. Miller, for his constant support, encouragement, and insights and for reading each and every chapter as it came off the computer.

Contents

Single Parents by Choice

A Growing Trend in Family Life

Introduction

We are living in radically changing times, and many of the norms and values of the recent past are in flux. The traditional nuclear family (father, mother, and children), long considered the mainstay of Western society, no longer represents the largest proportion of American households. In a span of a mere thirty years, the traditional family has gone from constituting 44 percent of all households in 1960 to 26 percent in 1990.[1]

While the traditional norms of the family, such as marriage, parenting, and family life, continue to be valued by most people, it is no longer the case that the majority of Americans will live in such a family for the major portion of either their childhood or their adult lives. Because many of the norms and rules governing family behavior have relaxed, in recent years we have witnessed the emergence of an unprecedented and growing number of alternate family patterns and lifestyles.

The purpose of this book is to examine one of these changes, namely, the growing numbers of single people who are choosing to become parents or to raise children while alone. Between 1970 and 1990, single-parent households almost tripled in this country, 3.8 million being recorded in 1970, and 9.7 million in 1990.[2] This book does not examine all such families. Much has already been written about the single-parent family characterized by low income and lack of education. Rather, the focus of this book is on those people who are relatively well educated, financially stable, and who have deliberately chosen to become parents or to raise their children while single: Who are they? What determined their decision? How are they managing? Of special importance, how are their children doing? These and other issues facing this growing number of nontraditional families are examined in the following pages.

We also need to ask how such changes could have come about in a society that has long viewed the nuclear family as the optimal setting in which to raise children and, by some, as a universal law of nature. In order to gain a better understanding of how such changes have occurred, we need first to look at some of the statistical facts and figures.

Major shifts in changing family patterns in the post–World War II period first started to occur at the end of the 1950s; many of them reached their peak in the 1960s and 1970s. The divorce rate, for example, more than doubled during that time. Whereas the divorce rate was 9.2 divorces per 1,000 married women in 1960, by 1975 it had risen to 20.3.[3] Although divorce figures reached a plateau during the 1980s and did not continue to grow at such a rapid rate, they have, nonetheless, continued to maintain this new, higher level.

Partly as a result of higher divorce rates, more American adults than ever before are now living alone and are anticipated to spend a significant proportion of their adult lives in a single status. In 1990, just under 23 million single-person households were reported in the United States, compared to 10.9 million in 1970.[4] In other words, over a period of twenty years the number of adults who were living alone more than doubled. Moreover, of those people choosing to live with a partner, increasing numbers do so before marrying, and many in the absence of marriage altogether. Couples who do decide to marry generally do so later in life, in some cases serially, and divorce earlier. A small but significant number of married couples are deciding to remain childless, and an increasing number of single people are deciding to have children. These include gays and lesbians— both as singles and as couples—who most commonly adopt or become pregnant through artificial insemination. In short, the variations in what constitutes a family today have exceeded by far our traditional definitions.

These changes have occurred not only in the United States, but also in many European and other Western countries. For example, births outside marriage in the United Kingdom were 54,000 in 1961, 139,000 in 1985, and 223,000 in 1990.[5] In France, a primarily Catholic country, in 1976 6.8 percent of all births occurred outside marriage, 12.7 percent in 1981, and 30 percent in 1991.[6]

With the recent opening up and democratization of Eastern Europe, similar changes are expected to be seen in some of these countries. For example, in Francine du Plessix Gray's 1990 book on Soviet women, many of the young women Gray interviewed expressed the wish to have children without necessarily anticipating the need to get married.[7]

More children than ever are being raised in single-parent households. Although this is primarily due to the growing numbers of divorces, as well as of unplanned pregnancies occurring outside marriage (in spite of the current abortion laws in most states, these figures have not decreased), a growing number of single men and women are electing to become parents. Between 1980 and 1990 while the figures for babies born to married women remained constant, those born to unmarried women rose by a whopping 64 percent![8] Although the majority of these births occurred among black and low-income families, an increasing number has recently occurred among white and higher-income women.

What these figures illustrate is the growing decline of the

centrality of marriage and its link to childbearing in our society. It appears that parenthood (as well as love) and marriage no longer go together "like a horse and carriage."

How did such major shifts in the fabric of the family come about?

The rapidity with which cultural, economic, and technological changes have occurred in the decades following World War II knows no precedent. In no peacetime period since the Industrial Revolution has society undergone such rapid shifts of norms, values, and lifestyles. Under the impact of postwar prosperity and such causes as the civil rights movement, the sexual revolution, and the women's and the gay rights movements, a wide array of new options and possibilities came into the public awareness and, in essence, have influenced the national character of this country. Turning away from a focus on the family, hard work, and self-denial based on the Puritan ethic, people began to search for and question the quality of their lives in new ways. With a growing preoccupation with self, they began seeking other means by which to find personal satisfaction and self-fulfillment. This search was to culminate in what became a cultural revolution.[9]

The years following World War II were a time of great stability for many Americans. In this period of prosperity and optimism, both marriage and the birthrate were at an all-time high. In the 1950s, approximately 44 percent of all households consisted of a nuclear family, the median family being a father, a mother, and 3.5 children. The year 1957 saw the highest birthrate in the United States recorded since 1917: an estimated 4,809,394 babies were born, or 122.9 live births per 1,000 women between the ages of fifteen and forty-four.[10] In a national survey conducted in the same year, 80 percent of both male and female respondents expressed the view that someone choosing not to marry was either sick, immoral, selfish, or neurotic.[11] By the late 1950s, this would all start to change.

The age of prosperity led people to want and expect more out of life, both spiritually as well as materially. Women had begun to get a taste of working outside the home during the war years, and they liked it. Growing numbers of women began to look beyond motherhood, and even marriage, in order to find satisfaction in their lives. The impact of living in an atomic age led yet others to question the viability of bringing children into a world that had a potential for self-destruction. Millions of people began getting themselves sterilized. During the zero-population-growth movement, which peaked in 1972, it is estimated that about ten million Americans were sterilized.[12] In the midst of expanding desires and expectations, both birth and marriage rates were beginning to plummet, and divorce was on the rise. Then came the economic reversals of the 1970s and the Vietnam war. For better or for worse, the cultural revolution was in full swing.

In 1976, in a twenty-year follow-up study on the Gurin *et al.* survey of attitudes toward marriage referred to earlier, only 25 percent now responded negatively to choosing to remain single, in contrast to 80 percent in 1957; 61 percent were neutral, and the remaining 14 percent viewed the unmarried state favorably.[13] In another survey, done in 1979, 75 percent of those interviewed considered it acceptable not only not to get married, but also to have children while single. In a longitudinal study examining views on childlessness, 82 percent of the mothers said in 1962 that all married couples who could have children should have them, whereas only 43 percent felt this way in 1980.[14]

Although there is clearly a greater acceptance today of couples who are opting for childlessness, there appears to be no rush toward its endorsement. Rather, recent trends appear to suggest a growing interest in the direction of wanting children.

Not only have significant changes emerged in patterns of marriage and the family, but with them have come a growing acceptance of diversity and alternative lifestyles. Whereas people choosing such lifestyles a mere two generations earlier may have been looked on as social deviants, these lifestyles are now being accepted by growing numbers of the population. Even many who would not choose such lifestyles for themselves have become increasingly accepting of others who are making such choices. More people are living together in the absence of marriage, and increasing numbers are cutting across religious and racial barriers in their choice of partners. Homosexuality has come out of the closet, and increasing numbers of gays and lesbians are now openly living together.

One response to these changes has been to view the structure of the family as being slowly chipped away, an occurrence that could only spell disaster, not only for the family, but for the very foundations of our national character. Because the family has long been considered the main transmitter of cultural norms and values, how would a breakdown in the very structure of the family affect our young people?

Another viewpoint has seen these changes as having a liberating effect, freeing the individual from the confines of the past. People now have the opportunity to shape their lives in ways not feasible for their parents. There is no need to live unhappily into old age in a marriage that has no redeeming features. Women can aim for the stars, with or without a man in their lives. If homosexuality is indeed an involuntary state, why be condemned for it? Many feel that, at least in some areas, America is becoming less status-ridden and more diverse, tolerant, and open-minded.

Yet, others feel that we have become amazingly self-indulgent and narcissistic, the "me generation." We are so inner-focused that we often exclude the needs and desires of other individuals as well as those institutions necessary to our well-being. We are, literally and metaphorically, "throwing out the baby with the bathwater."

Others are just plain confused.

Over a ten-year period, between 1970 and 1980, a national analysis of social trends examined how people were being affected by cultural changes. It found that approximately 17 percent of the population were actively involved in cultural change, whereas 20 percent were generally unaffected. As might have been expected, the remaining 63 percent majority was found to be somewhat in the middle, holding onto many of the traditional values, and at the same time embracing newer ones related to personal self-fulfillment. These studies also found that there was a strong increase in aimlessness, especially among the young.[15]

In his 1897 studies on anomie, the French sociologist Émile Durkheim described the breakdown in a social structure. This occurs when the usual mores and norms have collapsed, leaving people feeling that there is a lack of law and order, and that observing the rules of society makes no sense. As a result, a feeling of anomie, or normlessness, prevails, characterized by disconnectedness, depression, and isolation.[16] In seeking to extend the concept of anomie, Robert Merton has pointed out that deviation need not necessarily be threatening to the social system and, in fact, may be viewed as offering new patterns of behavior. Similarly, conformity is not necessarily functional.[17] Take, for example, the conformity of the German people in World War II. Although many complied with the prevailing rules of their society, one could not say that the murdering of millions was ultimately functional. New social patterns of behavior are usually considered a deviation from the norm until, or unless, they come to replace previously accepted patterns. At this point, they become the new norms.

New ideas are met initially with resistance. Few changes of any enduring cultural value come about without some kind of conflict, and it usually takes generations for new ideas to come to fruition. In the space of one or two generations, we have seen such a profusion of changing social views and behavioral patterns that we have not yet had time to fully integrate and distill them.[18]

According to Hannah Arendt's definition, a cultural revolution is not merely a change, but a special event that launches a society in a new direction. It disturbs the status quo so that the old beliefs, values, meanings, traditions, and structures are upset and profoundly modified.[18] If this is so, then we are, indeed, embarked on a cultural revolution!

We need time to see which patterns will last, adding to and enriching our society, and which ones will be abandoned, to fall by the wayside. In the meantime, the reality is that we have in our midst an abundance of new family constellations, in which potential parents make major decisions about how to conceive and raise their children. It is the intention of this book to examine some of these new family experiences so that we may understand them better.

We will be examining four groups of single-parent families: (1) single women who have became biological mothers; (2) single men and women who have adopted, including those who have adopted older children as well as infants; (3) divorced parents, including only parents, who have been either primary caretakers or very actively involved in the parenting role; and (4) gay and lesbian parents, who will be discussed separately because of the relative newness of the phenomenon of openly gay parents, although some of them may also fit into any of the three other groups.

Some of the things we will be looking at in connection with these four groups will be their own families of origin and their motivation for becoming parents. In addition, we will ask: How have their family and friends, as well as the community at large, responded to their unconventional choice of lifestyle? What kind of support systems have they developed? What is the history, both present and past, of their own romantic relationships? How do they explain to their children the absence of a second parent? And how are the children doing?

All the interviews are with real people, speaking in their own voices. In some cases, composites have been created, in part to disguise identifying data and maintain confidentiality, and in part in order to present the rich breadth of the material collected. Descriptive material was altered only when its inclusion would have too easily identified the interviewee. In rare cases, syntactical modifications were made if the meaning was not clear.

It has not been possible to write this book without going through much profound soul searching and reevaluation of my own belief system and values. Emotional neutrality is not easy when one is dealing with such a sensitive subject, which touches on social values we have imbibed with our mother's milk. When dealing with such material, there is a danger of becoming either prejudiced or overly compassionate, both of which I have, at times, been guilty of. Nonetheless, I have tried to deal with these feelings as they have arisen, and I hope that what I present here is as objective as possible. Pure objectivity, after all, does not exist.

Chapter 1

Why Single Mothers by Choice?

In recent years . . . the largest increases in nonmarital childbearing have occurred among relatively older women.
National Center for Health Statistics[1]

Single mothers by choice started to appear with some regularity in movies, fiction, and the popular press in the early 1980s. The first to be seen in a major feature movie was in 1983's *The Big Chill,* and the title character in John Irving's *The World According to Garp,* published in 1978, was the progeny of such a parent.

While the birthrate within marriage has been going down, the birthrate outside marriage has gone up and recently reached the highest levels ever recorded in this country. In 1989 alone more than one million babies were born to single mothers.[2] Moreover, a recent study that examined motivations for pregnancy found that, in the last decade, although fewer single white women were having unwanted babies, intended childbearing within this group had gone up.[3]

The overall birthrate among single mothers, which has grown fastest among white women, has increased 50 percent since the mid-1970s and has been particularly pronounced among older women. Whereas the typical childbearing age continues to be twenty to twenty-nine years, first births for women aged thirty to thirty-four have gone up 55 percent, and 48 percent for women aged 35 to 39.[4]

A number of relevant demographic and social factors must be considered at this point. First, because of the record high birthrates of the baby boom years the number of women aged thirty to forty-four in the population has increased considerably since the 1970s. Second, there has been a growing trend in recent years toward postponing marriage as well as childbearing. And finally, many single mothers are, in fact, cohabiting with the fathers of their child(ren) in marriage-like relationships.

More women than ever are, nonetheless, living alone, some of whom are electing to become mothers. This trend has been reflected by the health statistics of the United States Department of Health and Human Services, in which single mothers by choice are mentioned specifically.

> It is difficult to account for the rising trend in nonmarital childbearing by relatively older women. Presumably, many of these women have chosen to become mothers even though they are single. Data for 1986 on the educational attainment of mothers according to marital status suggest that although unmarried mothers are not as well educated as their married counterparts, still about 30 percent had completed at least 1 year of college and about 10 percent were college graduates. The incidence of mistimed or unwanted births among well-educated women would be expected to be relatively low. More research is needed to determine the factors associated with the rising rates of childbearing by older unmarried women.[5]

> It raises the possibility that the rising rates of births among unmarried women reflect deliberate choices to accept single parenthood.[6]

The Introduction presented an overview of the social changes that preceded the emergence of new family patterns. In the remainder of this chapter, we will examine some of the major factors contributing to the emergence of the phenomenon of single mothers by choice.

THE CHANGING ROLE OF WOMEN: WORKPLACE AND HOME

The emerging women's movement of the 1960s addressed itself primarily to the needs of educated, white, middle-class women. During World War II, when women were encouraged to go out to work as an act of patriotism, it was middle-class women who were experiencing, many for the first time, the novelty of working outside of the home. Poor women, after all, had always worked. For the first time in American history, not only were large numbers of married white women taking jobs, but women were outnumbering men in the workplace. When the war ended in 1945, women made up an unprecedented 57 percent of the work force.[7] Although many were working in low-level jobs or were making less money than men for the same jobs, the consciousness of these middle-class housewives was being raised by thoughts of new possibilities previously unavailable to them.

Women's staying home to devote themselves to *Küche, Kirche,* and *Kinder* was very much a product of the Industrial Revolution. Previously, women had frequently worked alongside men, sharing in producing the goods essential for the home. Sex roles were less distinct, and women shared a good deal of equality with men. Ironically, it was to take another economic transition, this time the result of war, to lead women to once again assume the role of provider, but now with a greater level of sexual equality.

After World War II, women were no longer needed nor,

indeed, wanted to fill the jobs previously held by the men, who were now returning from the armed forces. Although most women returned to their homes to produce the babies later to be known as the baby boomers, women continued to enter the work force in growing numbers, even though public opinion still generally disapproved of women, especially married women, working unless absolutely necessary. A working wife was often viewed as implying that the husband was unable to fulfill his designated role as provider. Hence, a wife who wished to work left many a husband feeling nervous.

As increasing numbers of women began to enter the professional schools and to receive more advanced job training, greater opportunities gradually started to open up for them. However, these tended to be at the lower end of the job hierarchy, and women earned less than men, regardless of their qualifications. Discontent with these inequities continued to grow, and as more and more married women left the home to enter the workplace, the women's movement, encouraged in part by the civil rights movement, began to reemerge from its dormancy since the period of the suffragists.

With the publication in 1963 of *The Feminine Mystique,* Betty Friedan was to articulate the question many had begun to ask, namely, whether the role of homemaker was sufficiently satisfying or fulfilling. Although not rejecting its importance, she urged women to look outside the home for additional opportunities to enrich their lives, opportunities that should, ideally, be equal to those available to men.

Under the impact of the burgeoning women's movement, many more occupational opportunities began to be available. In addition, as a result of the post–World War II inflation in the 1950s and 1960s, economic necessity rather than choice, forced more women to work. Women were concurrently asking more and more questions about the primacy of their homemaker roles.

With the greater availability of more effective forms of contraception and a loosening of the social sanctions against extramarital sex, the sexual revolution was also under way. Many women, especially those born in the postfeminist era, were beginning to question the need for motherhood, and others questioned the need for marriage. For a woman, climbing the corporate or professional ladder was demanding enough; to do so while raising a family seemed overwhelming. Many women decided to postpone marriage and a family until they felt they had reached a desirable level of professional success. Others felt that the imperative to marry altogether was no longer so important.

It was in this context that becoming a single mother became a viable option. It is noteworthy that it was the very children of the baby boom generation, children born at the peak of traditional American family life in the twentieth century, who were now making radical new decisions regarding the format of the family.

ILLEGITIMACY

Every known society has had some kind of structure or value system by which the status of children born into it has been determined. In most cultures, those "born out of wedlock"[8] were considered outside the law.

Although such children were referred to as bastards or as illegitimate, strict sanctions against them were rare before the time of the Reformation. Any sanctions were usually related only to matters of inheritance. A nobleman in seventeenth-century France, for example, was unable to pass on his title to illegitimate offspring but could openly acknowledge and socially accept them.

Following the Reformation, and under Puritan influence, the Church began to establish stricter controls over the institution of marriage. Sex outside marriage was increasingly subject to censure, and monogamous marriage came to be viewed as the only permissible outlet for the expression of sexual feelings. Women who engaged in illicit unions and their offspring were often ostracized and, as a result, suffered financial hardships. Even at that time, a double standard prevailed, as the men who fathered these children were not subjected to the same strictures.

The Industrial Revolution made it possible to accumulate huge amounts of wealth. In order to ensure that one's wealth would be passed on only to one's rightful heirs, sanctions against illegitimacy became even more stringent. Although such laws have always existed, there have always been segments of society in which they have been of little importance. Such subgroups have included the poor, the disenfranchised, and the artist, as well as those who have deliberately chosen to deviate from the majority culture.

Most literature on illegitimacy remained heavily moralistic until the development of the social sciences in the 1920s and the 1930s. With this development came a shift away from moralistic attitudes to one in which the application of psychological and sociocultural perspectives gained primacy.[9]

Crisis situations, such as wars, disrupt the normal running of any society and result in the weakening of many social norms. The first half of this century saw two world wars. Wartime family separations inevitably influenced the usual sexual practices, one result being that sanctions against intercourse outside marriage were weakened.[10] This, combined with the introduction of more effective forms of birth control in the 1960s, and the availability of safe and legal abortions did much to redefine sexual norms.

Women became relatively free of the fear of unwanted pregnancies, and the result was a greater degree of the sexual freedom formerly reserved for men. Sex for pleasure, rather than for procreation, gained greater acceptability.

More people began to question whether sex should be permissible solely within the confines of marriage. What had previously been viewed as a social deviation—namely, premarital and even extramarital sex—was increasingly becoming acceptable. The sexual revolution was under way.

Sex outside marriage, or adultery, is as old as society itself. Laws and sanctions never come about in a vacuum; rather, they are responses to actions deemed unacceptable by those representatives of a given society. Although such laws do not necessarily prevent such behavior, they do function as a brake or deterrent.

As social sanctions toward sex outside marriage were modified, it was, perhaps, inevitable that there would be an increase in the numbers of births outside marriage. Although these social sanctions still exist, children of unmarried mothers no longer have to suffer the social ostracism aimed in the past at children born out of wedlock. Certainly, today is a far cry from the days of Nathaniel Hawthorne's *Scarlet Letter.*

CHANGING SEX RATIO

The escalating birthrates of the baby boom years have had a dramatic effect on the sex ratio in this country. Prior to this period the male to female ratio was usually high; that is, there were more than 100 men for every 100 women in the population, as a slightly larger number of male than female babies is typically born into any given population.

The sex ratio is highly sensitive to demographic changes such as births, deaths, and migration. A significant reason for the historically higher numbers of men in the U.S. population is that more men have usually immigrated to this country than women.

It should be remembered that women typically select marital partners approximately two years older than they are. When the birthrate goes up over a period of years, there are subsequently fewer older men in the population relative to the number of available marriageable women. When it goes down, the reverse is true. During the peak baby-boom years of 1945 to 1957, the birthrate increased about 2.1 percent a year, resulting in an increase in the numbers of women in the population. To further compound this situation, in the years immediately before 1945, the birthrates were the lowest in recorded U.S. history.

The overall effect on women born during the upward trend of births, which continued into the mid-1960s, was that, as they reached adulthood, they were faced with a shortage of older men. For these women, there were simply too few men in the traditionally defined pool of potential marriage partners.[11] Whereas in 1940 the sex ratio was 101 men for every 100 women, by 1970 the ratio was down to 92 men per 100 women, and only 81 single men per 100 single women. Hence, many of the women from the 1970s on found themselves in a marriage squeeze that left them without potential partners.[12]

The most recent figures available indicate that, in 1989, there were 24.2 million unmarried women aged thirty and over in the United States, whereas there were only 14.5 million unmarried men in the same age group. Thus, the sex ratio is currently 60 single men for every 100 single women in the population.[13]

Further influencing this situation is the fact that women typically marry up in terms of occupation and education. Under the impact of the feminist movement, women were simultaneously outpacing men in educating themselves. Currently, women outnumber men in many of the professional schools, such as law and business. Therefore, fewer of the men available are reaching an educational level beyond that of most marriageable women. As a result, women at the upper end of the socioeconomic scale find the smallest number of suitable male partners available. One study by Neil Bennett and David Bloom predicted that one in five college-educated white women born in the mid-1950s would never marry.[14] While these figures were viewed as somewhat controversial at the time, they nonetheless bear some validity. As the title of an article written on the subject asked, "Where Are the Men for the Women at the Top?"[15]

Because of the downward swing in birthrates from the mid-1960s through the mid-1970s, the scarcity of males has finally started to reverse itself, so that among young adults now entering their twenties men are outnumbering women. This change, however, came too late for many of the women of the baby boom years who, given the option, would have chosen to marry.

THE BIOLOGICAL TIME CLOCK

The normal reproductive life span for a woman ranges from the age of fifteen to forty-four, the optimal childbearing years being ages twenty-five to twenty-nine. Not only were women of the baby boom generation faced with the marriage squeeze, but many found themselves racing the biological time clock. Many had also chosen to defer marriage and/or childbearing to pursue a career. However, when confronted with the biological deadline, many, both married and single, who had elected childlessness began to have second thoughts. Medical advances allowing for the early detection of fetal defects also played a key role in helping many older women to decide to have a child.

Until recently, it was improbable that a middle or upper-middle class woman would choose to raise a child alone, without the support of a husband. As we have seen, because of a wide range of factors, such women have now chosen to embark on the new and uncharted course of voluntary single parenthood. Let us meet some of them and hear their stories.

Chapter 2

The Mothers Themselves

*What factors go into this decision? Is it that
they are very healthy, or do they do it because
of childhood things, or in fact, is there just a
lack of eligible men to marry out there?*
A Single Mother by Choice

In spite of their growing numbers and increasing visibility in the media, the literature on older single women choosing to become mothers is relatively sparse.

A few self-help books have been written specifically for the potential single parent. In *And Baby Makes Two,*[1] Merritt and Steiner focus on the importance of having financial security and a good support system, as well as the possible legal implications involving the putative father. The authors interviewed over a hundred single mothers and found that many of them placed much greater importance on having a child than on finding a husband. In contrast to having a child, marriage was not seen as a necessary component to feeling fulfilled. Most of these women expressed satisfaction with themselves and appeared to have adapted well to the mothering role.

In *The Single Parent Experience,*[2] a book that includes issues geared to single males, homosexuals, and adoptive parents, as well as to biological single mothers, single parenting is viewed very much within a cultural context. The author, Carole Klein, feels that single parents are now a sufficiently large group to be significant in influencing future societal norms. She also feels that it is no longer necessary to link parenthood to marriage.

In their book *Up Against the Clock*,[3] Fabe and Wikler offer advice of a practical nature on how to juggle a career with motherhood. They also discuss what options are available for the single woman contemplating parenthood. *Out of Wedlock*,[4] an autobiography, describes the experiences of one single mother who felt the need to have someone special in her life.

RESEARCH STUDIES

A number of studies of single mothers by choice have tended to focus on the women themselves, rather than on the children. The reason is that, until recently, this group has been statistically quite small, and most of their children are still relatively young. As the children get older, no doubt more studies will be done on them. What follows is a summary of the relevant research literature, which, not surprisingly, has been done exclusively by women.

Although most of these studies are qualitative and were based on small samples (the smallest number of subjects was eight and the largest twenty-one), a profile emerges nonetheless. The single mother by choice is frequently a white, educated, financially stable, professional woman who may have a prior history of marriage and/or pregnancy. She usually comes from an intact traditional family, although the parental marriage may have been conflictual. In many cases, she was either the eldest or the only child in her family.[5]

One study found that, although the relationships with

their own mothers were generally positive, many of these women had negative relationships with their fathers, whom they experienced as emotionally unavailable and/or unpredictable. Many described their mothers as passive. The author, Mary Rexford, concluded that many of these women had subsequently developed negative attitudes toward men. No significant differences, however, were found in overall personality profiles when these women were compared with their married counterparts.[6]

Another study concluded that one of the motivating factors in the choice to become a single parent was a rejection of the passivity these women had witnessed in their own mothers, which they associated with the sex-stereotyped, traditional marriage of their parents. Although these women had felt special or different as they were growing up,[7] the Rexford study[8] suggests that they may have received subtle encouragement from their mothers to engage in nonconformist behavior.

A study that included psychological testing among its measures also interpreted the nonconformist choice of lifestyle as a reaction against repeating the kind of poor marriage many of these women had witnessed between their own parents. The authors saw these women as "pseudoindependent" and felt that many were dealing with unresolved issues related to feminine identity and intimacy.[9] I did another study that focused on the issue of intimacy and found that a number of women had described having difficulties in romantic relationships with men. Many were able to achieve closer and more trusting relationships in their friendships, whether male or female, than in their love relationships.[10]

In contrast to some of the above findings, one study found that mothers living alone with their infants were able to adapt to the maternal role more easily than mothers who were living with the fathers. The author felt that this finding challenged the notion that single mothers are unable to cope adequately without familial support.[11] Another study that questioned the accuracy of negative stereotypes of these women found that all of the women interviewed were intensely interested in becoming mothers and enormously committed to parenting their children well. Using in-depth interviews and a questionnaire, the authors concluded that these women were raising their children successfully. This study also conducted a survey that evaluated people's attitudes toward single mothers by choice. The authors found that men were generally more critical than women, and that the women who received the most criticism, from men and women alike, were those who had deliberately become pregnant without telling their partners.[12]

More often than not, single mothers express a preference for a baby girl. One study, however, found that postpartum depression occurred more frequently after the birth of a girl, in spite of the fact that many of these mothers had initially stated a preference for one.[13]

Although many single mothers deliberately plan their pregnancies, others do not. However, even when the pregnancy is "accidental," it is often, as one mother put it, "a subliminal choice." Because many of these women have experienced at least one abortion, one can assume that had they really wanted to terminate this pregnancy, they would have done so. Most of these women become pregnant with someone whom they have known for some time and whom they have told of their wish to get pregnant. Some have used donor insemination. A sperm bank in New York City reported a large increase in requests from single women and described these women as "bright, talented, superior women who refuse to settle for just any man in order to get married and have a baby."[14]

There is no single explanation of why these women choose to become parents while single, or of what method they use to reach that goal. Many of these mothers have clearly placed a greater value on parenthood than on marriage. Although some have seen the two as mutually exclusive and reject marriage, we shall see that, in most cases, the choice has been, rather, to become a parent alone or not at all.[15]

A PLANNED PREGNANCY

CYNTHIA, aged forty, is the mother of five-year-old John and lives in a cozy, roomy apartment in Brooklyn. The manager of a travel agency, Cynthia is an appealing-looking woman with a ruddy complexion, who impresses one as quietly self-assured. She is the eldest of three children, whose mother had been diagnosed as manic–depressive when she was a child:

My mother was a weak person and not to be counted on. I mothered the other kids. My father was strict and difficult to communicate with. They were a poor match psychologically, and I didn't have good role models in terms of a healthy marriage.

Cynthia was married while in her twenties. The marriage lasted for about two years:

I was content with the role of the housewife, but I started changing. I told him I needed him to share in the responsibilities in the home. He resented it and didn't want to do it. We went to a marriage counselor, but we eventually separated. I was very upset because I loved him, but I knew we wanted different things in our lives.

When I was nineteen, I got pregnant and had a child with a married man. The baby was given up for adoption. It was very big loss for me because I had always wanted children. When I was thirty-two I decided that I wanted to be pregnant, but that I didn't want to wait for Mr. OK or the biological clock. So I told an old friend of mine that I wanted to get pregnant. He agreed but did not want any responsibility, which was fine with me as I didn't want the relationship, but

I wanted a child. I named him after my father. My father died when I was fourteen.

Afterward I got terrified; it was such a huge leap. But it was the most wonderful thing I ever did in my life. My mother was very supportive; she was wonderful. I didn't think she had it in her because she was not a nurturer.

The key thing for me in being a single parent was just wanting to have a child in my life, to love that child and to understand what my priorities were. It's important to have a career, to make a bunch of money and do a lot of material things, but it's important to have someone call you "Mom." I believe that a lot of women in their thirties and early forties who don't have children are afraid to acknowledge that part of themselves because, very often, men are jealous of that.

I stayed home for several months, so there was the bonding with John. I was free to do whatever I wanted with my time, with my son; I had nobody telling me what I was doing was wrong. I had no conflict. I could devote all my energies to nurturing and mothering my child and have free time to myself. Not having a man around was fine, and I learned to juggle all those things. Whatever I needed to do, John went with me. I was just enjoying loving him and taking care of him, and if I didn't sleep at night, I slept in the afternoon. I didn't feel any pressures about having to cook dinner for somebody, or his wanting to go out Saturday night if I'd rather be home with the baby, or if I was too tired and he would feel hurt. So it seemed fine. I chose it that way, I guess. I created it, because if I had waited for Mr. OK to come along, I wouldn't have my son.

I feel lonely some of the time. My life is very happy and fulfilled, except for that part of it—a special man in my life to share the emotional times, the physical times, and for John to have a father. I'd like to have a loving, committed partner, being there for each other. I haven't attained that with a man to the degree I would have wanted to. As a result of my childhood situation, I was never able to depend on anyone.

Because as soon as I depended on someone, they weren't there. And that's a result of having an ill mother, and I understand that—children of depressed mothers and the problems they have with relationships. So I understand where my fears have come from, but I am still cautious about getting involved with somebody. I'm still not a hundred percent sure about marriage.

Since I hit my fortieth birthday, I feel I am very much in touch with what I want in a relationship. Really, for the first time in my life, I have been able to come to terms with the fact that I need a man in my life. I don't want to do it alone. I can do it all, I can work and own my own home, and have my child and have a social life and cook and clean and be superwoman. But I don't want to continue to do it that way. I'd like a man to see that I am not always such a strong person, but a woman who needs tenderness, caring, and support. I want to be able to depend on people more; I want to not be so independent.

I've only come to that conclusion recently. I got so caught up in being a total and perfect mother. I tried to give John everything two parents would have given him, all the boy stuff also. I probably didn't try to make time in my life to go out and have a romantic life; being a mother took precedence. But I feel as if I am at a different level because of John. These things weren't important to me before. I want a special relationship now, and I believe that it will happen.

JOYCE is a sociology professor who teaches in a midwestern college. She is thirty-eight, but her long, flowing blond hair and informal style of dressing make her look more like one of her students. Joyce grew up just outside Pittsburgh, the second of four children of a physicist father and a mother who was a housewife:

I had no thought about marriage at all in my twenties because I had been brought up to think that you finish your education first and get your career settled, and then you get married. I was twenty-nine when I got my Ph.D., and I thought it was time to think about having children and getting married. Only there wasn't anybody around for me to get married to. A lot of the other women I knew around my age were saying that they would have a child if they didn't find someone in a short period of time. So it was an idea that was in the air. I didn't realize that most of them were not all that serious and weren't going to do it. I also saw other women who were in their mid-thirties who were absolutely desperate to have a family, but they hadn't found anybody. I thought that I was never going to be in that state, where I would be desperate to find somebody to have kids with.

I am the sort of person who believes you run your own life. I decided that, as I had not found the man of my dreams at that point, I would start a family, and if I found a man later, he could catch up. So I suggested to George, an ex-boyfriend of mine, that he father a child with me. I had lived with him when we were graduate students and still liked him a lot.

We talked about it, and later he decided to do it. He said that he had discussed it with most of his friends, and they said it was a really bad idea. He said, after that, he just couldn't resist the temptation! Our expectations were not really clearly laid out. I said I would take responsibility for the baby. He could have whatever relationship he chose, but I had total control because I would be paying for the child. But there was this unspoken thing between us that we would perhaps move in together and see how things turned out.

It was not something we had really discussed between us. My relationship with George was something I considered apart from having a child. If we got together, it did not hinge on having the child. Even though it didn't work out, he does play an active role as a father. He lives in another state, but I would like it pretty well if he took a job closer.

The pregnancy was awful. I went into it totally unprepared. I don't think women are honest about what their experiences are like. I was totally wiped out physically.

Since Joyce wanted more children but didn't want to repeat the experience of pregnancy and childbirth, the second time around she adopted. Six-year-old Keith now has a new sister.

When Joyce became pregnant with Keith she had already moved away from Pittsburgh and has maintained little contact with her family.

My family had never been especially supportive. Both my parents were space cadets. My father worshiped my mother, but she sometimes got depressed and irrational. There were no rules in my house as we were growing up. I took care of the younger ones, I was the parentified child. George's family accepts me, and his mother helped out a lot after Keith was born.

Before, I had thought that if I had a child and I was the one raising him and I was a good parent, it would make absolutely no difference there not being a father in the house, that the child wouldn't miss it. That was before I had Keith, and I am surprised to say that that has changed. I am very glad that his father has a good relationship with him, because my son seems to be really close to his father. Even when Keith was very little and we would go and see George, when we left it would really tear me up because I could see that Keith missed having his father around. I did change a lot in my feelings about Keith and his father.

But I haven't changed in one thing. I do believe that one good parent who makes a good childhood for the child is as good as 90 percent of the two-parent homes I have come across. They have their own problems and their own agendas. The single mothers whom I have known who made a mature decision to have the kids are really concerned and involved. I would say that, in the ideal world, two parents who love each other and are doing a great job together would be better

than a single parent. But I still hold that a good, really
involved single parent who wanted to have the child is better
than most of the homes I have seen.

I feel sorry for many married mothers because they have
an additional problem putting up with husbands who seem to
make things more complicated. I don't see the married women
I know getting a better deal, getting enough support and
understanding. I think it's simpler to have nobody to blame
but yourself.

The hardest thing was the physical exhaustion, never
having time to think. But I have arranged a life that is exactly
what I wanted. Having children made me feel more centered
and settled in myself. I am doing a much better job than my
parents did. I am doing what I do best, raising kids.

When you're alone you can get very lonely and feel really
desperate, but when you've go kids, you never do feel that
lonely. Children can never fill the same niche as a boyfriend
or husband; it's just something they can't do. If you're any
kind of decent parent you don't rely on your children for that
kind of support but just for having somebody to hug you and
love you and all that stuff.

The worst reactions I have had about being a single
parent are from men. I was really surprised, because I expected worse reactions from women, but men, across the
board in every age group, really come unglued. I don't really
understand that, because it isn't like when I was raised, when
every house on the block had a father. Everybody in the whole
world is divorced today.

I miss having a relationship now, missing sex is the worst
part. I'm good in relationships; there is no one who left me; if
anyone left, it was me. I treat people very well, but I have
never met anybody who has been as good to me. The person
who will treat you the best is yourself. I don't want to have
anyone have control over me. Even if I were ever to get
married, I would want to have separate bank accounts.

It's very hard to explain, but I somehow suspected that I

would never get married and have a wonderful, happy relationship. I am so independent and strong. Maybe it's as simple as the fact that I don't need a man to support me. I know we are in a new age now, but men are still not very accepting of a woman who is really able to be that competent and successful. I think there was a certain amount of filling a void in my life by having children, in the sense that I didn't picture myself finding a man whom I could make a life with.

I asked her what she thinks will happen when her children are no longer there to fill that void:

It bothers me. It's like being in a boat and throwing the anchor overboard. You're still moving, but you're moving around the center. When they're gone, the cable will be cut, and the boat can go away. In one sense, I think of that as enormous freedom, but a part of me wishes that I had a longer time to be a family. It seems too short, but I'm not sure I'm different in that from any couple that has children.

AN ACCIDENTAL PREGNANCY

ANDREA, forty-five, is a real estate agent. An only child, she describes her parents as having had a pretty good marriage. She describes her mother as the dominant one and her father as being a gentle and loving man to whom she felt more connected. A somewhat heavyset woman with dark features who speaks in calm, measured tones, she is the mother of eight-year-old Stephanie.

When I turned thirty-six, suddenly reality was there. But I knew that if I didn't marry, there were other options. Adoption was not so comfortable for me. It was complicated because there were lots of sick kids. I tried to get pregnant and wasn't able to, and then I got pregnant by accident. I'm usually very regular and it was past my ovulation. The father was someone with whom I had been in only a casual relationship, and he was shocked when I told him. I offered him as much or as little involvement as he wanted. I told him there was no pressure, no strings. I've had no contact with him since, and Stephanie has never met him.

She has asked why she doesn't have a daddy. I told her that when I became pregnant I really wanted to become a mommy, but her daddy didn't want to be a daddy. She asked why, and I told her that some people want to be daddies and some don't, that it's a big decision. It comes up periodically, the same question, maybe twice a year. My feeling is that she will be struggling with the meaning of that until she is twenty or maybe thirty, that it does not really mean as much to her at this age as it will later on. She's beginning to get it. She's begun to understand the concept that I was never married. She didn't get that for a long time; she didn't understand that single meant never married. So we had to go through what single meant. That was another phase.

I worry about Stephanie growing up without the other parent, but thus far, I don't see any problems. Her godparents are my closest friends, and the man in the couple is our male role model. He comes over once a week, which is very important to her. I had thought it would be easier to have a daughter, but on reflection, I'm not sure that it has been. I think girls, in many cases, have as much need for fathers as boys do, a place to learn how to develop a relationship with the opposite sex in an intimate setting in the family.

Andrea's father had already died before she became pregnant. Her mother, although initially shocked at learning of the pregnancy, was thrilled at the prospect of becoming a grandmother and became very involved in taking care of Stephanie. Andrea was able to plan her work schedule around Stephanie's needs and also had a large network of friends:

A lot of my relationships with friends have to do with having a child, women who are mothers and the children are friends also. I have friends who may or may not be mothers, and they are a very important part of my life. My friends are my support system.

The thing that has been the most difficult is, not when times are hard, but when times are good. Something wonderful happens, your kid does something wonderful, and there's no one to share it with. To turn to someone else would feel like bragging. Also, I wonder about her having to deal with the pain of not having a father. I know I had a wonderful father, and sometimes, when I walk down the street and see a kid with his or her dad, it hurts me that she will never have had that experience.

I'm not dating now; it's not a big priority in my life. I am not feeling lonely or needy. I am very busy. I had a relationship two years ago that left me pretty devastated. He was very involved with Stephanie, which I regret deeply. Looking back, we never got past the honeymoon phase, and when we hit difficulties, the whole thing fell apart.

Since I have had a child, I realize that it's not easy for me to share my life with somebody. I had never really understood that before. Having Stephanie has helped me be more able to do that. There's no question that my capacity for intimacy has grown. It had to; otherwise I would never have been able to get my relationship with my daughter on a positive basis.

I didn't realize before how comfortable I had been meeting my own needs and not having to meet somebody else's. All of a sudden, there was this little creature who had no inkling that I had any needs. It was quite a confrontation at first to realize that I had no choice. The fact that my child was not a man who could disappear made me have to deal with issues that I had never really been forced to deal with before. I couldn't say, "OK, you can leave now; I am going to find a better daughter." I had to stretch, grow, do whatever I could and get grown up pretty quickly.

I think I tried my best to meet her needs, and I learned there were rewards in doing that, which I had never experienced before. No man ever stayed around long enough for me to have to deal with that. Either they would leave or I would leave when things got uncomfortable or difficult. It was just too easy. Relationships tended to be too disposable, especially before AIDS. With a man, you could say, "He's not meeting my needs, and there's another man out there who might be better."

Looking back, if I had the skills I have now, I know I would have had a man in my life then. There's not a shred of doubt that I can get through tough situations with people, where, before, I would just have ended the friendship, woman or man. I don't want my relationships to be disposable anymore. I would really prefer to have a partner. It doesn't have to be a spouse. I used not to look for commitment; it was not a concern to me. I think I was the problem in the men I picked. In the past, the fear of being left by a man made me too submissive. Being left is not such a big issue anymore, because I have somebody; I have Stephanie.

EMILY, fifty-one, is a free-lance writer, the oldest of a large, comfortable, middle-class southern Episcopalian family. Seated in her worn, yet comfortable apartment and speaking with a soft southern drawl, Emily has the flavor of a 1960s bohemian.

The most important thing for my mother was her family. On the other hand, she suffered the way a lot of women did from being intelligent and educated and having ideas of things she wanted to do. She got back on track when I was fourteen when she started working. My father basically liked her independence and was very supportive of her.

Emily was married while in her early twenties. Both she and her husband were career-oriented, and neither was eager to have children. In any case, Emily did not see herself as the maternal type. Thirteen years into the marriage, Emily got a job that involved a good deal of traveling. Shortly after, her husband decided that the marriage was not working:

It could have been my establishing some independence that made him realize that it was not a good marriage after all. I think he needed something from me that I was not interested in giving. I was comfortable with the idea of each of the couple doing their own thing, but that was not really his way. We did try to work it out for a couple of years. The divorce was relatively calm and civilized in a way, no hard feelings. But after fifteen years, you come up empty.

A month after the divorce, I just got pregnant. I didn't use birth control this one time. I am sure it was deliberate on one level and that the divorce was directly involved in my getting pregnant. So here I was. I knew very early, before my period was late or anything. It was somehow different. I had not been eager to have children—I was not even good at keeping a plant alive! But my first reaction was, "what a good idea!"

I had had an abortion when I was nineteen, and I thought I was going to go through with an abortion. Then I decided not to. I realized the only reason to have an abortion was because of money, and I decided never to do anything ever again important in my life for money.

The father and I were in a casual relationship; he was someone to run like a rabbit if anybody put any requirements on him. He didn't want anything to do with it at all. I was relieved because we were not a pair, and it was clear to me that this was really my thing. I also felt basically that any life I could provide would be all right. I was confident in the essential areas. I had lots of emotional energy; I was free.

My mother's first thought, which she expressed the very first minute after I told her, was that she didn't want to wind up taking care of this child. She was terrific after, though. My father said that it would be nice if it had not been a mixed blessing, but he was very sorry that abortion had to be considered. My sisters, on the other hand, said that they could fully understand my wanting to do this.

After Ethan was born, I went down to stay with my folks for a couple of weeks. I didn't have to work right away, and for the first few months after he was born, we established a schedule that was entirely dependent on the baby's needs and mine. I remember noticing that I didn't have to worry about a third person's nine-to-five schedule or whatever; I just didn't have to think about that. So whatever was the schedule was the schedule for the two of us. I nursed him until he was about two. We were very close during those bonding years, and I think that's very important if you can arrange it. Money was an issue, and I didn't have much help. Sometimes, I had some pretty young baby-sitters, and I remember one saying, "Oh, she's adorable." So I knew she hadn't changed the diaper!

A good proportion of the single mothers interviewed breast-fed their babies, many of them well into the second year. Figures on current breast-feeding practices in this country indicate that just over half of all newborn babies are breast-fed, and that the majority, 81.2 percent, are not nursed beyond their fifth month. According to these figures, single mothers seem to breast-feed beyond the usual norm, at least for this culture.[16]

Emily continued:

I met John just before Ethan was born. Even though we split up when Ethan was four, and John is married, Ethan has regular contact with him. He was never economically or legally responsible, but he often wound up helping. Their relationship was established very early, and the biological father is just not important at this point.

I wondered how Ethan had felt about this. Also, as he was older than most of the other children of the mothers I had interviewed (Ethan was almost thirteen), I wanted to know more about how he was doing. I had met Ethan earlier, as he had wandered through the living room during the interview. A well-built, articulate, and outgoing youngster, he had been fascinated by our discussion, had stayed for a few minutes, and then had gone off to visit a playmate.

I remember when he was real little and John was reading a book to him, which referred to a daddy. Ethan piped up, "Well, first Mummy had me, and then we needed a daddy, and we looked around and found you." I couldn't have put it better myself! When Ethan was about eight, he did go through a period of feeling rejected and being curious about his biological father. Apparently he wrote in something in a class at school that he really would like to meet his father, because his father would like him. At that point, we talked some about that and how his father's not being around had nothing to do with him.

Ethan is rather shockingly boylike. When he was little I tried to expose him to the entire range of possibilities. I wanted him to grow up to be nurturing, and I gave him dolls to play with as a child. He, of course, immediately identified with everything male-oriented on television, wanted books about guns, and like to watch war movies. Either he's naturally a boy, or he's overcompensating for not having a father.

When he was six or seven he became very physically expressive with men. I felt he really needed that contact. If he was with a man, he would wrestle with him or just be physically close. Now that he's older and with his peers, that need has disappeared. I can't see in his particular case that this has been a problem for him. Ethan is a very positive and secure kid. He's methodical, never the foolhardy type, sometimes slightly cautious.

Every one of his friends is from some different family combination, and I just don't think that's an issue for him. One of the things he is spared that children of divorce go through is the fighting and using the child as a crowbar on each other.

Being a single parent is not an issue in my life. My concerns for my son are no different from anybody else's. I recommend parenthood, and as stress-free as possible, and sometimes that's being single. I still can't help thinking that it would be best to have a family arrangement that was a marriage—a good solid marriage and a few children. However, failing that, the next best thing is not a bad marriage, but no marriage. So single parenthood is not a bad second to a superb marriage, and a poor marriage is a poor third.

I asked how important a relationship was to her at this point.

I am pretty sociable, and it could happen. But since the time of my marriage, when we were together longer than we should have been, I have felt that I wouldn't have a relationship that didn't have somebody having a separate domicile, at least as part of it. Somebody having separate roots somewhere, just so that people didn't get claustrophobic. But Ethan and I have a very comfortable way together.

DONOR INSEMINATION

JULIE, forty-one, has a master's degree and works as an administrative assistant in a large public relations firm. A rotund, cheerful-looking woman wearing a bright sequined sweater, she wastes no words, speaking directly and to the point. Julie was born in New York and is the only child of Jewish immigrant parents.

My parents had a fairly good marriage. My father was quiet and very easygoing, but my mother was very assertive and not at all warm. I never had a particularly good relationship with her.

I was married very briefly when I was thirty. He was younger than I and very immature. I had always thought I would have a traditional marriage, but it didn't work out. I had also always thought I would be a mother. I had a lot of love to give, and when I got to my mid-thirties, it became a real need. There was no man in my life at the time, so I decided to get artificially inseminated. It was very well planned and best because there would be no legal problems or child custody battles. It was also easier for my parents to accept. My mother was very supportive, but my father didn't talk to me for the first three months! Now he's come full circle.

Jennifer was born by cesarean section. Cesarean births, which account for about 25 percent of births nationwide, appear to occur rather more frequently among older single mothers. Although this high percentage may be accounted for by the age factor, medical experts have expressed the view that this procedure is often performed unnecessarily. This assertion raises the question whether single mothers may be more vulnerable to or at greater risk of inappropriate medical practices than married mothers:[17]

I had some income saved and was able to stop working for the first couple of years. Becoming a mother changed my whole lifestyle. It's a lot of work, and I don't have much free time. It's financially hard, and I find myself being jealous of two-income families because, if I were married to a man who was making as much as I am making, we would have a very fine life. I am in a very high income bracket for a woman, and I still find it's a struggle. But I would do it again in a minute.

When she was about three, Jennie started asking me about having a daddy. It's really very difficult; it was hard to explain this to her. One person told me she said there are all different kinds of families and we're mummy and a baby. I decided it was best to say that she had a daddy, but that we don't know him. I'm still not clear on this, but as she gets older I will tell her the truth.

I have become friends with a lot of married women who

have children, because now we have similar interests, and I have my single friends, whom I do things with socially. Before I had ever had my daughter, I had traveled to Europe and done all the other things I wanted to do, except have a good marriage. I guess I didn't attain the ideal, but I don't feel as if it was my fault. I'm pretty satisfied with what I do.

If I had it to do over, I would have done it earlier and been married. I date a lot, but I would like to have a relationship. I had been seeing a recently divorced man and would have liked something to come of it, but he wasn't ready for a commitment. I just think I haven't met the right person, or it hasn't been the right timing for him. But I must say it's not that important to get married anymore. Before, there was that need and urgency because I wanted to have a child. Now, if I don't ever get married, it's OK, too. My life is complete. It doesn't depend on a man to make me happy.

A PRIVATE MATTER

BARBARA works as a secretary in an accountant's office. A petite, somewhat sad-looking woman of thirty-nine who speaks in a deep, husky voice, she nonetheless has an easy and outgoing manner. The oldest of three siblings, she speaks fondly of her mother, who died last year:

My mother was a saint, a beautiful, wonderful person. My father was a gentle-looking man, very meek outwardly, but he beat my sister and me. I disliked him enormously. My mother was very unhappy and burdened with three kids, but she stuck out the marriage because of finances.

Barbara was married in her mid-twenties to a man who was a drug addict. She was not aware of his addiction until after the wedding, but she hoped she could help him overcome his problem. Within two years, he died of an overdose:

I haven't had problems meeting men, but for whatever reason, I have found over the years that I don't know how to play the romance game. I realized that I just couldn't figure out how to make a relationship work. I can't blame it all on the men; obviously, it's me, too.

About six years ago I had decided to be celibate. It was a decision I was very happy about, but two months later, I met Jimmie's father, so that was the end of that. He was ten years younger than I. He seemed like a nice person and was physically attractive. I liked him but didn't love him. I had always wanted a child, and I was tired of waiting for the right situation to fall into place, so I went for it. I stopped using birth control; I planned it and didn't tell him. In two months, I was pregnant. I never told him, and to this day, he doesn't know about Jimmie.

My mother was in seventh heaven. She said, "Well, you won't have a man to take care of as well as a baby." My father was OK, but later he was thrilled to be a grandparent.

I stayed home the first year to take care of Jimmie and then put him in day care. The adjustment to infancy was enormous because of the lack of sleep, but my mother helped out a lot. There was always the drudgery of daily life: laundry and cleaning and cooking and organizing and trying to rest, because it was so exhausting. My main difficulties were the compromises in my lifestyle and fear of failure as a mother. But I accomplished something that had just seemed out of reach for me. My hopes were for this permanent connection of love and care for the rest of my life, not to grow old and be alone. Looking back, I would still have made the choice, but I would have waited until I had saved some more money.

I have a whole bunch of new friends who have children; naturally, we gravitate to one another because we have children. I am not as fluid as I was before, but we manage to keep up. I had sworn I wouldn't become a homebody just because I had a child, plus it's more difficult than I had thought, plus I don't have so much money to pay for baby-sitters. I really regret that I can't do as much as I used to. The social outlet that I have is the telephone these days.

I used to put a lot of store in seeing men, but I really don't find it as important as I used to. I really find them terrified of taking me on; they are interested in sex, but not interested in commitment. I don't want to introduce a whole series of men to my son; I don't really like that revolving-door situation. I'm not exactly a spring chicken, and men must view me as someone who comes encumbered. They have to share my attention with Jimmie; he comes before any man.

I did have a boyfriend for a while who lived in another state. We used to see each other every three weeks, and then we lived together for a while. But we got on each other's nerves, and we didn't always agree about my son's discipline. At one point, he wanted to marry me. It was at a time when I had been struggling very hard, and I convinced myself that I loved him and would marry him. Then I realized, to my shock, that it was because I wanted his help—I wanted him to take care of me—and that the only advantage of having a husband would be the money.

Many of the women who made the decision I made— maybe it might be important to know their feelings toward men in general, maybe their fathers. I believe that my father and the physical abuse had a great deal to do with my decision underneath, that maybe it wasn't so important to have a father in the house. Maybe if I'd seen my father as this wonderful, terrific man, I might have thought, well, gee, every family has to have one of these. But it just didn't seem to be a prerequisite to a family.

I would like a relationship if it didn't drain me and drag a lot of my energy away from me. It's got to be a relationship that is supportive and actually frees me, but I haven't been able to find that.

Surprisingly, Jimmie, who is now five and has been attending nursery school for almost a year, has never asked questions about his father. When he does, Barbara says she plans to tell him the whole truth.

RACHEL, *aged fifty, lives in a university town in the Boston area and is the mother of five-year-old Jessica. She is a slender women with dullish brown hair. She has a scholarly and somewhat somber look, uses no makeup, and wears horn-rimmed spectacles. Rachel earned her doctorate in biology and currently teaches at a private high school. The middle of three children, she grew up in the Washington area, where her father practices law and her mother is a housewife. Rachel was once married for nine years. As she starts to talk, she becomes more animated.*

We had tried to conceive while I was in graduate school, but I couldn't. Then I found out that my husband was involved with someone else. I was very hurt, especially that he had lied to me. The divorce was traumatic; that's why I didn't remarry. I felt very unsure of myself, as if I was untethered. I went through my thirties in a fog.

I very much knew that time was clicking away and that I wanted to have children. I also wanted a companion, but I didn't want to start another relationship at that point because I was burnt out. I did live with someone right after the divorce, but it was a relationship chosen specifically because I knew it wouldn't last. When I was younger, I had never had to go looking for men, and now it made me feel very uncomfortable. I wanted to, but I guess I didn't quite know how to go about it. In any case, most of the men I know who were available were either fresh out of a divorce or were older and had grown kids.

My parents were symbiotic; their relationship was not made in heaven. They got along with each others' neuroses very well, but the dynamics were very unhealthy. I think it's why I chose the husband I chose. I didn't choose somebody who loved me very much. There were other men around who loved me a lot, and I didn't choose them. I've got some problems I have never worked out right, that somehow complicate my relations with other people.

I waited until the very last minute, biologywise, because up to that point I was hoping to do it in a more traditional way. But that would have involved both my meeting somebody who was appropriate and my readiness. I was also very concerned about whether I was able to conceive, but the fact that my mother had had my brother late in life gave me hope.

It was really more spontaneous than planned out. I had a relationship with somebody and simply allowed myself to conceive. He didn't know. When I told him, he was very unhappy. I gave him the option of being involved, and he definitely didn't want to. I realize there was a lot of dishonesty there, and I shouldn't have done it. It was a profoundly selfish thing to do, probably the most selfish thing I have ever done, but I haven't regretted it for a moment!

The only person in my family I told was my sister. I was terrified to tell her; she was the big sister and much more conservative in lifestyle than I am. She's married and has grown children. I am still in awe of her a little. Her response was "That's a gutsy thing to do," which was exactly the support I needed. I decided that, if there was a big problem with the fetus, I would abort, so I waited until after the amniocentesis to tell my parents. My sister's advice was to bite the bullet and tell them, and I knew that I had to either go forward or make peace with not doing it.

When I called my mother and told her, there was silence for a second, and then she said, in a very sad voice, "Oh, I know you want children, but I can't be happy about this." By the time I went down to visit the following week, she was already talking about her granddaughter. She really wanted another grandchild, and that took precedence over whatever shock and concerns she had had about how I was going to handle the situation. My father was thrilled and completely accepting from the minute he heard it.

As far as my teaching position was concerned, I knew

legally they couldn't touch me, but the administration was wonderful. I expected a certain amount of distancing, especially from the strongly Catholic and staunchly religious ones on the staff, but I found myself very much taken care of by people. My biggest supports were my friends and family. My single friends who don't want children have been so affectionate and responsive, too, it was a surprise—although, right after she was born, my focus was so totally on the baby that some of my friends didn't understand. It was difficult for a while, but they're still there.

I had some wonderful responses from my students, boys and girls alike, and many of their parents sent me presents. I remember going in to tell the first group of kids. I was so nervous. After I told them, they applauded, and I started to cry.

I had enough money saved, and I took a year off. After that, I put her in day care. I nursed for nineteen months. People said it would be difficult taking care of a child by myself, but I think I may have had an easier time doing it by myself. The physical problem was not a real problem for me; I am very organized and competent. I would like another person to take some of that responsibility, but there's something about relying on somebody. There's a strength in independence that somehow when I am in a relationship gets very muddled up for me. In the reverse, I love the dependency of my child. The dependency is clear and it's fine and I love it. She's getting very independent, and I am enjoying that process, too.

The positives are watching her grow, the discovery process. Feeling the love for a child is infinitely more interesting than I would ever have imagined. There's something about the interaction; it's a growth experience. I would have liked to have three children. I have grown emotionally tremendously, and my relationships have changed with men since Jessica. I am drawn to men who are very different in my estimation from the men whom I was drawn to before: family-type men,

men who are softer. I would love to get hooked up with someone. I feel I have a better chance than ever before because I feel so much happier.

My interests and priorities have changed completely. I am not as career-oriented as I used to be. I am not as absorbed with myself. It makes me feel good that I have someone to take care of. It gives me a certain sense of purpose. I always felt a kind of desperation, and that's not there anymore. I feel more content. I am just much happier.

The negatives are the exhaustion, and I worry about money and my health. I am the only one she has. Before I had Jessica, I worried, what if she got sick in the middle of the night, what was I going to do all by myself? Also she is being raised without a father, and I guess that saddens me. I mean, I don't idealize the nuclear family, but I see how fathers are, and I have to get straight about it in my own head so that I don't impart any of those feelings to her. To the best extent possible, I want her to feel secure and to feel that I am secure.

She gets along well with men. Her main role model is my father. Her teachers say that Jessica gets along as well with the boys as with the girls. She started asking questions when she was two, and I told her that there was a person who was her father and that he had helped put her in my tummy, but that he wasn't part of our lives. I think single mothers really don't know what to say. That was one of the most difficult things to figure out, what to tell her. I really wanted to be able to give her an answer that would be OK with other people.

I think there will be some anger with me. She says to me now, "I wish I had a dad," but I think this will come up more fully as she gets older. Jessica came home upset from school one day recently. Her teacher had asked the children to draw a picture of their families. Jessica had drawn a picture of herself with me and Jeff, a man whom I have been seeing lately. She is pretty attached to him and told her teacher that he was my friend. The teacher said that a mom and a kid and a friend weren't really a family. I think it would be really helpful if teachers acknowledged more the fact that not all children are growing up today in families that have a mommy and a daddy, and they should be more aware of and accepting of that.

SINGLE MOTHERS BY CHOICE

The New York–based organization Single Mothers by Choice (SMC) was started in 1981, after a newspaper article appeared describing the experience of one woman who had made this decision. Having grown from a small, informal group of ten women, it now has a membership of a thousand to fifteen hundred nationwide, with five hundred to seven hundred in the New York City area. SMC does not present itself as an advocacy group; rather, its philosophy is that, although a good marriage is a preferable situation in which to raise a child, single motherhood is a viable option. It offers its members and their children a variety of programs, including social get-togethers, lectures, and study groups, and it provides a wide range of resources. It also offers thinkers' meetings for women who are in the process of considering whether to become single mothers.

I met with Jane Mattes, the founder and director of SMC. Jane, a single parent herself, is also a psychotherapist:

The society in which we live has such poor interpersonal skills. Some of the people who choose to become single mothers have difficulties with intimacy and have said that they were so desperate for a relationship that they drove men away. But it seems to me that you can have real difficulties with intimacy even when you are married. I know plenty of couples who are having a hard time. In the past they would have been much faster to split up, but they are not so ready to do so now, not when you have to worry about getting a deadly disease.

I agree with her that being married per se does not rule out the possibility of having difficulties with intimacy. I also wonder whether married women with such problems tend to be overly needful of attachment, whereas single mothers with these difficulties tend to express them in overly independent behavior.

Jane Mattes says: We talk about this intimacy question a lot in our meetings. Almost everybody who has had a child seems to be more introspective. They are aware that having nobody in their lives was tempered once they had a child. They weren't as needy, so that they could then handle a relationship with a man better. I think having a child makes them better able to handle the ups and downs, the closeness and distance within a relationship. Work and relationships take on a different perspective; everything takes on a different perspective. Having to work this out with a baby helps one to work this out with a man.

I asked "What about the children?":

The women have to look at what they are doing to the child. It doesn't necessarily mean they are going to use the child. Any of the things we are saying can happen in a marriage. Married couples can also use their children—and do. You've got to have certain skills to hold onto yourself, or this baby is going to take you over.

This goes back to child-rearing problems. Because she is an analytically oriented therapist, I asked Jane what she thinks about the developmental, particularly oedipal, issues for a child growing up without a father:

It seems to me that children may have a harder time resolving oedipal conflicts with a mother where there's no rival. I can't say too often that women should try to recruit a man into their lives, not necessarily for themselves, but for their child, as some kind of important person. The world is half men and half women, and there is a need for a man to be involved with the child in some intimate way. My hypothesis is that otherwise the rival may be work. But we'll have to see when they grow up.

SUMMARY

There is no single formula for women who have made the choice of becoming single mothers. Although many in our sample described having had negative feelings toward their fathers as they were growing up, an equal number described having felt closer to their fathers than to their mothers. No single family pattern prevails. Most of these women are both independent and intelligent and have achieved considerable success in their careers and professional lives. They are personable and have been able to develop strong and lasting friendships. They are sensitive and thoughtful and all too aware of the potential pitfalls that confront them and their children. They are also highly committed to their role as parents.

A common theme that emerged was that many of these women did not feel satisfied with their relationships with men. This was an area where they had not succeeded in achieving the same degree of success as in other areas of their lives. A romantic relationship was seen by many as potentially threatening, as something that would deprive them of their independence and autonomy, and thus as something to be avoided or handled with great care.

Erik Erikson, who, perhaps, more than any other in our time, drew attention to the issue of intimacy, made intimacy the sixth of his eight developmental stages, immediately following "identity versus identity diffusion." A central task of adolescence, he defined intimacy as

> the capacity to commit to concrete affiliations and part-
> nerships and to develop the ethical strength to abide by
> such commitments even though they may call for signifi-
> cant sacrifices and compromises.[18]

I would add my own definition.

> the capacity to engage in a deep, committed and em-
> pathic relationship over time with another on whom one
> can depend, a relationship which can, but does not have
> to, include a sexual component, in which one is open to
> share personal information and able to adjust and modify
> some, but not all, of one's own needs in the interest of the
> needs and wishes of the other person.[19]

Some of the women I interviewed said that they did not particularly miss having a romantic relationship in their lives and that they led full and rich lives, enhanced by a sense of closeness to and intimacy with their friends. Shere Hite[20] suggested that women today are, in fact, experiencing less emotionally satisfying relationships with men and are gener- ally turning more to other women, rather than to husbands and lovers, in order to meet their emotional, as opposed to sexual, needs. Yet, the majority of those I interviewed ex- pressed a clear preference for being romantically involved.

Many of these women felt that the experience of mother- hood had immeasurably enriched their lives and had also enabled them to develop more mature relationships with men. Is it possible that, once they had experienced an intimate relationship with a child, they were able to find a relationship with a male peer less threatening?

In her article "Parenthood as a Developmental Phase,"[21] Therese Benedek, in essence, added a further stage to Erik- son's developmental schema. She pointed out that parenthood can offer a mother, or a father, an opportunity to work through previously unresolved psychological issues through the development of their relationship with their child. She suggested, for example, that the experience of becoming a mother inevitably reactivates earlier experiences with one's own mother, which, as in the stage of adolescence, may provide an additional opportunity to rework previously unresolved issues.

Although such maturation may well occur in many cases, the question of what effect these mother-only families have on their children still remains unanswered. This question was posed by one single mother:

> The thing that has always bothered me is: How harmful is it to a child to grow up without ever seeing a happy relationship between two members of the opposite sex? I grew up in a family where my mother and father never fought. They never had anything bad to say about each other. They stayed married, but they never seemed to be connected. If I had anything that I could put my finger on and say, "Maybe this is why I never did find someone who I knew I wanted to be with," it was, possibly, because I didn't see that growing up.
>
> And to what degree will my not having a man in my life affect my son's ability to find someone and mate? I would wish for him to have a loving relationship. Gee, wouldn't it have been great if I could have settled for that! I never could. I was too eager to go out and tackle the world.

Chapter 3

Single Parents by Adoption

Adoption is never simple, not once.
Adoption Lawyer

A lot of adoption is serendipity,
a matter of luck and where you are.
Single Adoptive Mother

Adoption is a theme found in ancient history as well as mythology. Some examples from the Bible are Moses and Esther, and examples from mythology are as diffuse as Oedipus and Superman. Children's classic fairy tales are replete with instances of stepchildren, Cinderella, Hansel and Gretel, and Snow White, to name a few.

In his paper "Family Romances,"[1] Freud wrote of young children imagining themselves to have been adopted, and that their "real" parents are of noble birth. Creating a second set of parents helps children to cope with their feelings of both love and hate toward their parents which usually coexist side by side. The second parent who appears so frequently in children's literature, often in the form of a wicked witch or stepmother, is an expression of this early fantasy and coping mechanism. If optimal development is to occur, it is important for the parents, as well as the child, to reckon with these feelings.

53

There are two sets of parents in all adoptions, one connected to the "wanted" and the other to the "unwanted" child. The parent(s) wanting the child may have to deal with infertility, often accompanied by feelings of loss or inadequacy. The parent(s) giving up the child must deal with an unwanted pregnancy and being either unable or unwilling to care for the child. All adoptive children must deal at some time with these two sets of parents—both in this case being real rather than one in fantasy.

HISTORY OF ADOPTION

In earlier periods of history, certainly before we became a so-called child-centered society, adoption was looked on as primarily serving the needs of adults, a medieval definition of adoption being "a legitimate act imitating nature for the solace and comfort of those who have no children."[2] In contrast, the focus of adoption today is the welfare of children who need a home.

Because adoption did not exist in English common law, it had to be created by statute. No adoption laws existed in the United States until the middle of the nineteenth century. Before then, children who had no parents were either placed in an almshouse or orphan asylum, indentured, or apprenticed. Texas is believed to have been the first state to pass a law dealing with adoption, in 1850. Massachusetts passed a statute the following year that not only established guidelines for adoption, but also became the model for other states' adoption laws. These guidelines made explicit that the child's welfare was to be the primary concern in adoption. They also required that the biological parents submit in writing their agreement to relinquish the child, and that the judge issue a decree deeming the adoption to be "fit and proper."[3]

In order to provide additional protection for the children,

Michigan passed a law in 1891 that required that an investigation be made before any adoption could be finalized. A 1917 law in Minnesota stipulated that a detailed investigation, followed by a written recommendation, be conducted by a local agency—hence the creation of the requisite home study. By 1929, every state had some kind of adoption legislation on its books.[4]

Later, requirements were added, such as a trial period before the adoption is finalized and a stipulation that records be closed and sealed after the adoption and that a new birth certificate be issued. In recent years, as increasing numbers of adults who were adopted as children have insisted on their right to access to their birth records, there has been a growing shift in the direction of open adoption or at least easy access to these records.

Agencies specializing in adoption were first established shortly after the turn of the century, and the first adoption standards were published by the Child Welfare League of America in 1959.[5] These are updated every few years. Following is an extract from its most recent standards, published in 1989:

> Child welfare agencies have a responsibility to provide preparation, counseling and support on an ongoing basis for all the parties involved in an adoption.
>
> The placement of children for adoption should have as its main objective the well-being of children. The needs of the child should be the primary determinant of the total service.
>
> It should not be the main purpose of an adoption service to find children for families, and it should not be expected to provide help for many of the problems associated with childlessness.
>
> Child welfare agencies have a responsibility to recruit families that are of similar ethnic and racial background to the children . . . In any adoption plan, however, the best interests of the child should be paramount.[6]

Although informal adoptions have always existed, adoption typically occurs within the context of a marriage. For married couples, adoption is rarely a first choice; rather, the decision follows a period, sometimes of years, of unsuccessful attempts to conceive and give birth.

Although the actual percentages of women experiencing infertility problems have not changed, their numbers have increased because of the following two factors: (1) since the baby boomers reached adulthood, there have been more women of childbearing age in the population, and (2) as increasing numbers of both men and women have delayed having children, there has been an increased likelihood of conception and birth complications related to age.[7]

In contrast to adoptive couples, for most singles adopting children adoption is the first choice, as the following comments illustrate:

> When I was a teenager and I used to get my dolls from around the world, I always felt I wanted to adopt. I never felt this desire to have a baby—ever. Adoption always appealed to me and was my first choice once I decided to bring a child into my life.

> Adoption was my first choice mainly because I had a problem with being pregnant alone. What would I do if I got sick?

> I thought if I was going to do it alone, it would be even harder if I was pregnant. I also felt that my need to have a biological child was not that great.

> It never occurred to me to have a biological child. I decided at twelve that I would adopt if I became a parent.

> There was a whole bunch of issues against getting pregnant, like going a few months without an income.

> There are so many unwanted children in this world, I thought it was unconscionable to bring another child into the world just to have a child.

> When I was much younger, I always thought I would

adopt children. Talking to other adoptive parents, I found that, for some reason, they had the same dreams and aspirations.

HISTORY OF SINGLE ADOPTION

Before the mid-1960s few, if any, children were formally adopted by single parents. Because it had long been the view that a two-parent family was best for an adoptable child, adoption agencies did not consider unmarried people suitable candidates.

The 1950s and 1960s saw many changes in adoption practices in this country. Until then, most children available for adoption had been the illegitimate babies of white middle-class and upper-middle-class women. As fewer healthy white infants became available because of the legalization of abortion and more readily available birth control, the focus shifted to the children who were entering foster care in ever growing numbers. An effort was made to extend adoption services to these children, with particular emphasis on children with special needs, or so-called hard-to-place children. Special-needs children are defined as being older, members of a racial or ethnic minority, siblings, or physically, emotionally, or mentally handicapped.

In order to deal with the limited availability of suitable adoptive homes for these children, the range of potential placements was expanded to include both single and interracial families.[8] One of the earliest efforts to place a significant number of children with single parents occurred in 1965 after the California State Department of Social Welfare revised its adoption regulations to permit single adults to become adoptive parents. In December of that year, the Los Angeles Bureau of Adoptions (now the Los Angeles County Department of Adoptions) placed its first child in a one-parent family. By 1967, it had placed thirty-nine children in others.

These families were evaluated two years later (in the first study of its kind on single adoptive parents), and both children and parents were found generally to have made a good adjustment. The evaluators described the parents as an emotionally mature group of people who had demonstrated a special ability to love and give to a child. Although still holding to the premise that a two-parent home was preferable, the agency concluded that a stable single-parent family was better for a child than the impermanence of foster care, and it recommended that qualified single adults be accepted as applicants to become adoptive parents.[9]

It should not be surprising that the least preferred children were placed with the least preferred families. Nonetheless, subsequent studies on single-parent adoptive families, which are few in number, paint a tentatively optimistic picture. This optimism, combined with the growing divorce rate, which has left more and more children living with a single parent, has resulted in some adoption agencies' modifying their attitudes toward potential single adoptive parents. However, most agencies still see single adoption as the placement of last resort and put such applicants at the bottom of their waiting lists. As a result, unless they are prepared to take a special-needs child, singles tend to opt for independent—that is, private—or international adoption.

Although healthy white infants are still the most in demand, regardless of applicants' marital status, singles tend to show a greater willingness to adopt special-needs children. The majority of single parents seem to work in such fields as education and social work, so that they may be more amenable to adopting, and perhaps more qualified to deal with, children who have special needs.[10] In fact, it has been suggested that, for certain handicapped children, a single parent may even be preferable. The following case is one such example.

MARGARET, *aged forty-five, is an ebullient heavyset woman who grew up in a large lower-middle-class family and has been working as a nurse for over twenty years. When I visited Margaret, she was plodding barefoot around her cozy apartment, with Jason, eight months, in her arms. Jason, a smiling and responsive infant, has Down syndrome. I also met Margaret's daughter, Janice, aged sixteen, who is moderately mentally retarded.*

I worked as a nurse in a hospital with children with handicaps, and my preference was for a handicapped child. These kids needed a home more than normal kids, and I had so much that I could give to a handicapped child, why would I want a normal child? When I first set eyes on Janice, she was already eight, but she was the size of a five-year-old and virtually nonverbal. But there was something so appealing about her that I just knew that this was my child.

If one did not know that Jason had Down syndrome, apart from the slight creases in the corners of his eyes, one would be hard put to know that he was not a normal baby.

In general they are easier, more placid, but he will have delayed motor development. He is not sitting yet and will probably not walk until he is two or three, but he is very alert.

This was not surprising, as Margaret was constantly joking and playing with him while he was awake. I asked her what it was like being the mother of two handicapped children.

I guess there's such a fulfillment. There is frustration, but the accomplishments are so great because you know that, without you, they might not have taken place.

Information available on adoption in the United States is rather limited and affects only a small fraction of the population. The actual numbers of adoptions have declined in recent years, with estimates suggesting that in 1982 there were 2.2 percent in the population who had ever adopted, compared to 1.7 percent in 1987.[11] Single adoption is legal in every state and increasing numbers of single men, as well as women, seem to be adopting each year.

TRANSRACIAL ADOPTION

Almost greater than the issue of single adoption has been the issue of transracial adoption. In contrast, interracial adoption first became a phenomenon in this country in the 1950s after the Korean war, when people were encouraged to adopt Korean children fathered by American servicemen.

With the increased efforts to place special-needs children in full swing in the 1960s and 1970s, many of these special needs children were being placed with white families. This trend was inevitable, as historically there has been an overrepresentation of black children in the child welfare system. Although many black families have been willing to adopt, they have been far outnumbered by white families.

The term *transracial* is sometimes limited to the adoption of black children by white families. Between 1960 and 1976, more than 12,000 such adoptions were recorded.[12] Many people saw this as a solution to dealing with the vast numbers of children without permanent homes, whereas others questioned the efficacy of placing black children in families that would be unlikely to reinforce their black heritage. In 1972, at the first annual convention of the National Association of Black Social Workers (NABSW), a statement was made expressing strong opposition to these placements, which were viewed as undermining the black community.

This statement had a major impact on adoption policy in this country, and transracial adoption continues to be controversial. As a result of this statement, many agencies revised their policies on transracial placements. One viewpoint was that adoption agencies were not being aggressive enough in seeking out potential black adoptive families and were, in fact, often discriminating against black families wanting to adopt. Another view was that there were simply not enough black families to meet the needs of all black children who were waiting. Moreover, it was felt that a stable white family would be preferable for a black child to remaining for years in foster care.

In 1978, in response to a nationwide effort on the part of white-adoptive-parent advocacy groups, the NABSW published an update of its earlier position paper on transracial adoption. Although not rescinding its earlier statement, it nonetheless somewhat modified its opposition to transracial adoption as being an attempt to undermine the black family and black culture.[13]

This issue remains unresolved, and many agencies do not permit transracial adoptions. Inevitably, the ones who suffer are the children. According to Mary Beth Seader of the National Committee for Adoption in Washington, D.C., there are approximately 360,000 children currently in the foster care system, 38 percent of whom are black. Ms. Seader states:

> We get calls daily for kids with special needs. There are enough families willing to adopt them, but most public agencies will not allow whites to adopt black children. There is definitely a bias against adoption in the system, and the children got lost in the shuffle. Some wind up in the foster care system for years and often develop attachment disorders, when what they need is a stable environment. The child welfare system is just too overloaded.[14]

That the foster care system appears to be either unwilling or unable to negotiate children out of the system and into adoptive homes has been heard over and over again, from both potential adoptive parents and professionals in the field. Whatever the reasons, which are admittedly complex, tens of thousands of children are left without the stability of a permanent home. Many of the single adoptive parents interviewed for this book were, in fact, prepared to take a special-needs child and initially tried to adopt through the system. Almost without exception, they gave up after months and, in some cases, years of thwarted efforts. Many finally adopted foreign-born children who were, ironically, transracial.

The following comments illustrate the experiences and reactions of these adoptive parents:

> Despite all the problems, there are people who are willing to take these children on, but they get very little help in dealing with them. There are not many support services.

> I made some attempts at domestic adoption, but I didn't get the services, and the child certainly didn't get the services. I had taken on a teenager, and when she began to have serious emotional problems, I asked the agency for help. But there were no services available. We were left to our own devices.

> I went to a meeting for singles, and I found out that, of a hundred people, one person had adopted through the system. Everyone else had adopted internationally.

> I did not get one referral from the Blue Book.* I was prepared to go up to age ten. No one tells you the truth. I felt that these public adoption agencies wanted your name on their records to show they were trying to get parents, but not one of them ever gave me a potential placement.

> I contacted a lot of agencies, and they all said, Come. The fact that I was single wasn't a problem. I went to see the Blue Book every month, selected a child, and sent in an application, but I never got a single response. It took me five years to go through that process.

> First I tried through domestic. I was told that, given that I was willing to take an older child, kids would be

---

* The Blue Book provides a listing of all special-needs children in New York State who are purportedly available for adoption, and it is updated every few weeks. It includes descriptions of waiting children, which are accompanied by photographs. Although this is no doubt a necessary procedure, the idea that children can be selected through a catalog is a chilling thought.

available. This was absolutely untrue. I sent out my requisite home study to the different agencies, and nothing ever came of it.

I was interested in adopting from the New York State waiting-children list. I took courses for six months and had my home study completed. Every two weeks, I went through the updated Blue Book. If I saw a child I liked and called the agency, I was typically told I was not the right color. I was very disillusioned.

According to the rules, if a child was handicapped, he or she could be adopted transracially. But they made such inappropriate referrals. How could you place a child in a wheelchair with a single mother!

As long as the children are in foster care, the agencies get paid. Once the adoption occurs, they lose their money.

I think America doesn't take care of its children. If there were more supportive services, more people would want to adopt in this country.

The adoption and foster care world is a machine that destroys people's lives.

In spite of the experiences described above, transracial adoptions do still occur.

TRUDY is a high school teacher. A petite, bohemian-looking woman of forty-eight, she adopted Brian two years ago when he unexpectedly became available as a boarder baby, which means that his mother had given birth to him in the hospital and was not going to take him home with her. Trudy is white; Brian is black.

I had been thinking about adoption for a year and a half before I decided to go to a nontraditional private agency. I hadn't started out to adopt a black baby, but he was available, and he was a well baby. At that point, I made the decision that I could deal with having an interracial family.

When you adopt a child of a different race, especially a

black child, you give up a lot of your white middle-class privileges. You have to think where you are going. If you are going to take a vacation, you have to think, are there going to be any interracial families there? You really have to have in your mind whether your child will be comfortable. What I could be comfortable with as a single individual, as a white person, even though I might not like the values, I can no longer do. Now I have an obligation to my child. It's actually tailor-making your life in some way. I didn't do it for that reason, but, when it comes down to it, that's what it is.

Although there are many people like Margaret and Trudy who are willing to adopt children who are either handicapped, older, or of another race, most people planning to adopt are looking for a healthy infant who looks like them. Because most private agencies who will accept single applicants usually place them low down on the waiting list, most singles choose either independent or foreign adoption.

INDEPENDENT ADOPTION

Before embarking on any adoptive search, one must take some necessary first steps: A preadoptive home study prepared by a licensed social worker must be completed, to evaluate the appropriateness of the applicant and to screen out those who are either psychologically and/or financially unsuited. In addition, fingerprint clearance by the Federal Bureau of Investigation is required to confirm that the prospective adoptive parent has no current judgments related to child abuse or any other criminal record. For certification as a preadoptive parent, some, but not all, states also require a personal screening, which usually entails a very brief court appearance before a judge. When adopting a foreign child, it is necessary to go through the United States Immigration and Naturalization Service. Since the Joel Steinberg case in 1988, considerably more bureaucratic procedures have been introduced into the adoption process. Although some are useful additions, others both add to the plethora of paperwork and, ironically, fail to prevent a possible reoccurrence, as Steinberg's "nonadoption" of Lisa was outside the law.[15]

The costs involved in adoption vary enormously and are influenced by such factors as whether the biological mother has medical coverage and how much is necessary to spend on travel and advertising. The total costs for independent or foreign adoption are usually between $15,000 and $20,000, although they may be less. There is also the gray area inhabited by unlicensed "baby brokers," who work outside the law and charge exorbitant and undeclared fees for locating an infant. Hearings were heard in 1987 on a bill, sponsored by Senator Robert Dole, entitled the Anti-Fraudulent Adoption Practices Act, but it died in committee and has not been reactivated.[16]

If one decides to adopt independently, the usual practice is to advertise, typically through a lawyer or a private adoption agency. When adopting through a lawyer, the potential parents place the advertisement themselves with the guidance of their attorney. In the case of agency adoption, it is generally the agency's responsibility to locate a birth mother or a child. However, in recent years, birth mothers have become increasingly vocal about participating in the placement of their children and, as a result, have been less willing to place their babies through adoption agencies. Whether the reason is a growing feeling of entitlement on the part of women or the move toward more shared information, if not open adoptions, some adoption agencies are now agreeing to permit parents to locate a birth mother themselves. Many birth mothers prefer this arrangement, as it gives them more opportunity to learn about the adoptive parent and to have a larger part in the selection process. This combination of independent and agency adoption is referred to as *identified adoption.*

Although only a very small percentage of adoptions today

are fully open, there is a definite move in the direction of more shared information between the adoptive parents and the birth mother and, hence, the child. Increasing numbers of adoptive parents are willing to maintain an ongoing relationship with the birth mother, although through a third party, such as an attorney. However, most adoptions taking place today are still closed.

Small-town newspapers, often in the Midwest or Southwest, are favored places for advertising, in which a potential single mother may offer a "loving home" as opposed to "loving parents" to an infant or child. Typically, the unlisted number of a telephone installed for the sole purpose of receiving calls from birth mothers accompanies the newspaper ad. After some rapport has been established with a birth mother over the telephone, she is asked to contact a lawyer (or an agency, in the case of identified adoptions), who then takes over the necessary investigations and legal arrangements. Once the adoption has been finalized, the telephone is disconnected, so that the birth mother cannot trace the child.

The laws governing independent adoption vary from state to state, but it is considered legal in all states except Connecticut, Delaware, Massachusetts, Michigan, Minnesota, and North Dakota.[17]

CLAIRE, aged thirty-nine, comes from a closely knit Italian family and owns her own office-supply business. Pale-skinned and petite, Claire speaks in an expressive and vibrant voice that belies her size. She adopted Anthony, now eighteen months, when he was just a few days old.

I decided international adoption was out because I couldn't deal with going overseas to collect a child. It was not my thing, and my family couldn't deal with a biracial child, so that narrowed it down. I decided I would give myself nine months, and if nothing happened, I would start donor insemination.

I met with a lawyer, and I started advertising. The ad ran,

"Loving home awaits your child. If you are thinking of giving your child up for adoption, please call this number collect."

You have to find out from the newspaper how many other ads are running. The first time I ran an ad, there were twenty-five others running. After that, I would call the newspaper first. If there were not more than six ads running, that was OK. The ad cost a dollar a line, and I would run it for thirty days. If you are not careful, you can spend thousands of dollars in advertising. I was careful and spent about twelve hundred dollars.

Within the first month, I got a very good potential response. She would not have an abortion; she was Catholic. She was very gung ho, and I spoke to her every week at her job. And then one week I called, and she was not there. I was told she had had the baby and had decided to keep it. I was devastated. Some hospitals will do everything in their power to convince the birth mother not to give up the baby. If you have a good adoption lawyer, he or she will steer the birth mother to a hospital that will not do that.

The next time, Claire was luckier. She got a call from a fifteen-year-old girl living in Nebraska who later gave birth to a baby boy:

I went to pick him up and went to court there. If you adopt in another state, you have to go through what's called an *interstate compact.* I never met the mother, but I have a form she filled out. I know her last name, and I know which school she went to. I don't want her to find me, but I would like to be able to find her. I can only speculate about what she must have felt.

INTERNATIONAL ADOPTION

Inevitably, finding a foreign child is considerably more complicated than undertaking a domestic adoption. One needs first to register with the U.S. Immigration and Naturalization Service. In order to have a file opened there, one must provide a dossier of documents, including birth certificate, a home study, a fingerprint check, documentation on marital status, and references on employment and financial ability. The adoption of a foreign-born child requires visas and naturalization, as well as the approval of the foreign court and the United States.[18]

International adoption is in a constant state of flux and is subject to the political climate in the given country, as well as its current relationship with the United States. The availability of foreign adoptive children tends to be cyclical. As orphanages in a given country become overwhelmed with children, the country's laws regarding foreign adoption may be relaxed. Agencies and lawyers then move in and set up the necessary adoption framework. At some point, rumors may emerge regarding scandals or illegal activity connected with adoption procedures, resulting in the laws being changed, and the doors slammed closed to foreign adoption. Although they may be reopened at a later date, the process usually starts over again in another country. This pattern seems to occur every few years, examples being Romania subsequent to its 1989 revolution and, more recently, Poland following the fall of Communism.

Children adopted internationally frequently come from underdeveloped countries that have both a language and culture different from those of the United States. Once an adoptive child has been found (it is rarely a newborn), the completion of the paperwork necessary to get the child out of the country can take months and, in some cases, years.

As with domestic adoption, it is possible to adopt a foreign child either independently or through an agency.

STEVEN is thirty-eight and is the principal of an elementary school in Upstate New York. A tall, bearded man who is slightly balding, he speaks in a somewhat reserved, yet relaxed and easy manner. Steven adopted his two sons through an agency that places children from Brazil.

When I was growing up, I had always thought of orphanage kids; I thought that I could provide love to these youngsters. I definitely did not want an infant, I wanted a kid who was already functioning.

First, I tried to adopt domestically through a public agency. Finally, I found a kid who seemed to be reasonably well functioning—most of the waiting children have such baggage. I took him preadoptively, and he seemed to do well for the first few weeks. Then, he started having problems. I later found out that he had been in eight different foster homes and that he had also been hospitalized for psychiatric problems. I had to force the agency to reevaluate him, and it finally determined that he was too disturbed to be adopted. The agencies just don't know about their own kids. It was horrible.

I heard of an agency that was open to singles and that worked with children from Brazil. I contacted this agency, and after it got my home study and I sent a fee, it sent me a bunch of videos. I saw these two brothers, aged nine and ten, who were living in an orphanage because their parents had abandoned them. My wish was to have a large family, and I thought, if these two little people had bonded to each other, they could bond to someone else.

They were taken to court and talked to about being adopted by a single male. They were also prepared by a psychologist at the orphanage. I had to make a scrapbook for each of them with pictures of my parents and siblings, my car, and my home. These were sent to the agency, which translated them and sent them to Brazil.

Six months later, I went to Brazil to get the children. I remember driving up to the orphanage and getting out of my car and being tackled by this big kid. I was totally taken by surprise. The younger one couldn't take his eyes off me. They started absorbing from Day One. It's amazing. They fit right in to their new life beautifully from the start.

Independent adoption is usually done through a foreign lawyer and/or a facilitator.

CHARLOTTE is a forty-five-year-old lawyer and the mother of seven-year-old Tanya. She is a somewhat serious-looking woman wearing a navy business suit and a starched, white blouse, and her black shoulder-length hair has just a tinge of gray:

No agencies in 1985 would even talk to me because I was single. I had thought of advertising but was told it was very expensive and very tough for young girls to imagine that another single woman could do what they could not imagine themselves doing.

I tried leads in Costa Rica, and I lost a little girl there because her mother changed her mind. I experienced it as a miscarriage and was very upset. I had also paid her money. I put things on hold for a few months, and then I met a person who has contacts in El Salvador. She had an arrangement with a lawyer there, and I knew she brought in healthy babies. She had just heard from the lawyer that there was a little girl in El Salvador waiting to go and asked did I want her, and I said yes. It is usually harder to get a girl baby, and I knew I really wanted a girl. Then I started waiting. I had thought it would take six months, and it ended up taking nine.

And then I was in El Salvador, standing in downtown San Salvador with my baby in my arms. I spent a week with my lawyer going to court. Everything that could be a problem was a problem, but I had this wonderful baby. Her mother had given her up because she had other children and had to go back to work. I know the mother's name and I know the town. The whole thing wound up costing me about fifteen thousand dollars.

A lot of people say something like "Oh, she's so lucky," but I feel that I'm the lucky one. People give you a halo because they think it's the most wonderful thing adopting a needy child, which is quite preposterous, unless you are Mother Teresa. You adopt a child for the same reason that you give birth to a child: selfish reasons to enhance your life.

Chapter 4

Single Adoption: The Parents

I feel there are a lot of people like me, my age, who focused on a career and who feel the need for a child. The reason why we're not married is, I think, that we have problems with intimacy, but it's mixed.

Single Adoptive Mother

Even though single adoption began to emerge in the mid-1960s, very few studies have been done on this subject. With the exception of one longitudinal study that was completed in 1980, no other studies addressing single adoptive parents have appeared since the early 1980s. What follows is a brief review of the research done to date.

In the studies describing children placed by the Los Angeles Department of Adoption in 1965 (referred to in the previous chapter), most of the parents were black women adopting either black or biracial children. This was also the case in a similar study[1] done in Chicago in 1976, which looked at twenty-eight women and three men, all of whom had adopted infants. Although the authors were struck by the diversity among this group of parents, they found them to be overall well educated, competent, and having a high capacity for nurturing. Although most had expressed the desire to have a child they could take care of, teach, and guide, some had expressed the wish to adopt in order to fill a void in their lives.

The authors of the article, Shireman and Johnson, categorized these parents into three groups according to their parenting styles. The first group were "superparents," warm, stable, and invested in their families. The second group were the "isolated" parents who, although enjoying parenthood, centered their lives on their children. The third group were the "demanding" parents, who were perceived as unable to offer much emotional support to their children. In a three-year follow-up of eighteen of these families, only two of the children were found to have emotional adjustment problems. The authors concluded that many of these parents had much to offer their children, while others were seen as at high risk.

In a study[2] in which the subjects were predominantly white women, who had adopted privately as well as publicly, data were collected by means of a mailed questionnaire. The mean age of the mothers at adoption was thirty-five. Most of these women were highly educated and had above-average incomes, and almost all said that their decision to adopt had been motivated by a wish to fulfill their own needs. Some were members of single-parent groups, which they described as having been very supportive, and many others wished that such a group were available to them.

In another study using mailed questionnaires, Feigelman and Silverman[3] compared a group of single adoptive parents with couples who had adopted. Of the sample of fifty-eight single parents, fifteen were men. The authors found the single parents to be more highly educated and to have higher status occupations than the couples, although not necessarily higher incomes, mainly because most of the couples had dual incomes, while the single parents were dependent on a single income.

The single adopters frequently lived in urban areas, working in fields such as education and social work and were more likely than couples to adopt hard-to-place children. This choice was seen as a reflection of their choice of profession in which they tended to be more exposed to children in need in their daily professional lives. More singles than couples, especially the men, described having had negative experiences in the adoption process.

The single parents reported significantly more emotional adjustment problems than did the couples, particularly when adopting older children. Because a greater proportion of the singles were professionally qualified to identify emotional problems and were more likely to have adopted troubled youngsters in the first place, such a finding might have been anticipated.

The extended family, for both couples and singles, played an important part in determining how long it took children, as opposed to infants, to adjust to their new homes. Where the extended family had been both accepting and supportive of the adoption, the children adjusted much more rapidly than when such support was not available. Support from friends was also important, but less so.

The authors concluded that the experiences of single and married adoptive parents showed more similarities than differences. While stressing the need for further work in this area, they also suggested the need to reconceptualize current theories of child development:

> Many of these theories maintain that two-parent families are indispensable to successfully resolve the Oedipus and Electra complexes, to offer role modeling opportunities, and to ensure the intergenerational transmission of cultural values and conforming behavior patterns. Most of the theories positing the inherent need for the two-parent family were conceived, however, during the early and mid-twentieth century, at a time when sex roles were far more differentiated and segregated than is true today.[4]

Over one hundred black adoptive children were the subject of a longitudinal study[5] that spanned fourteen years and included in its sample traditional, transracial, and single families. Although the single parents had had the most difficulty in discussing the adoption with their children, the overall adjustment of these children compared favorably with that of the other groups. The researchers noted that although the parent–child bond in these families had been unusually close during the latency years, in early adolescence (which is as far as the study went) developmental tasks related to separation and differentiation seemed to be progressing unimpeded.

In his overview of the problems and advantages of single-parent adoptions, Kadushin stated:

> Just as the two-parent family is not necessarily and inherently a nonpathogenic family, by the same reasoning the one-parent family is not necessarily and inherently a pathogenic family. Given the heterogeneity of single-parent families, some kinds of single-parent families will be more likely to be pathogenic than others. . . . To modify an old folk saying, lack of a father is not as bad as having a father is good.[6]

Although the term *transracial* is sometimes used exclusively to describe the adoption of black children by white parents, it is being used here to refer to all situations in which the racial background of the child is different from that of the parent. Many such transracial adoptions were included in the studies described above. In general, the research on transracial adoption has found little difference between these children and children adopted by parents of the same race.

A longitudinal study conducted by Simon and Altstein,[7] comparing 206 black adopted youngsters with their white nonadoptive siblings, found no difference in self-esteem scores of the two siblings. The authors concluded that, in order for the adoptive sibling to develop a positive self-image, it was of primary importance that their parents have positive attitudes in dealing with their child's racial heritage.

In another study that used mailed questionnaires,[8] Feigelman and Silverman studied a sample of 713 families that had adopted black, Korean, Vietnamese, or Colombian children. These authors found that white parents adopting black children were more likely to be upper-middle-class and liberal, whereas parents adopting children from the other ethnic groups were more heterogeneous. Black children generally encountered more racial hostility than children coming from other ethnic groups, and most children assumed a double ethnic identity: that of their own ethnic background and that of their adoptive family. When emotional difficulties were dominant, these were often traceable to preadoptive experiences.

Although not negating the complexities inherent in transracial adoption, the research literature generally presents a picture suggesting that a family offering both strong parental support and a positive attitude toward the ethnicity of the child can provide a beneficial environment for such a child.

ADOPTING AN INFANT

CLAIRE, thirty-nine, and the mother of Anthony, almost two, was herself born to older parents, the middle of three children:

My parents were both forty when I was born, but they did a lot with us, took us to the zoo, museums. I thought it was a bit weird that all my friends' parents were so young, but it didn't seem to be a problem. My father was very loving and was a big part of our family. My parents also loved each other very much.

Claire's father died twenty years ago:

I'd been involved with someone a long time ago for about six years. Neither of us could make the decision to tie the knot, and he finally married someone else. That is my one regret and definitely colored my decision to have a child. I wanted to have his child. I was in love in the truer sense, and I wanted to have our child together.

I woke up one day and said, "Wait a minute, if I don't do something, I will have another big regret of never having been a parent." I had been in love and had had the desire to have a particular person's child, but I didn't have any great need to see my own genes replicated. I saw a child as two steps. There was the outgrowth of a loving relationship, and then there was the parenting, and I was able to divorce the two. I said, "If it can't be a loving relationship, it doesn't mean it can't be a parenting relationship."

I can almost pinpoint what happened. I was meeting lots of men, but I didn't meet Mr. Right, and I met lots of wonderful women who were also alone. I woke up one morning and said to myself, "I can't wait to have another man in my life that I want to have a child with. I'm going to go ahead and be a parent myself."

I went to an Adoptive Parents Committee meeting. I had always envisioned that they would never allow a single person to adopt, and when I saw thirty or forty single people who had successfully adopted, men and women, I realized it could be done.

My siblings were very supportive, but my mother was against the whole idea. Although our relationship had been very good, it got bad over this. My mother would not even come over the week I got Anthony. She actually didn't visit for three weeks. Then she sat down with him in her arms and fell in love with him!

I have developed a network of other mothers and that's been invaluable. I also have a few very close friends I can rely on. Because of my business, I can sometimes work from home. Motherhood must be natural, because I was fine. Immediately, I went by gut feeling; it was just there. I learned very quickly to sleep when he was sleeping. Everything is the best; it has just been so wonderful, and he became an integral part of my life immediately. To be honest, I actually think about another child; I would love Tony to have a sibling, but not just yet.

I would still love to have a relationship. The ideal situation is to have a loving relationship and a child. But there are so many families now that are split up and mixed that being single is not enough reason not to have a child. Having my own business I think scares men off. You would be surprised how many men freeze up when you say you run your own business. My guess is that it's threatening. I see how they react, how they are often taken aback.

In the last few years I've run into men fifteen and twenty years older who are divorced and are attracted to the idea that I am independent, which is a twist. I am obviously very different from their ex-wives, and they don't want to be involved with a clinging vine again.

The hardest part is when you come home after you've really had a rough day, and if he's cranky, it would be really nice to have somebody else to hand him over to. But that's always going to be hard. It's harder to meet people, but it's really interesting how people come up and talk to you when you have a baby.

Anthony has male role models; my brother and my friend's husband are there for him. Although I would love to have a relationship, I think that I am adjusted enough, and if I am reasonable, he is not going to be maladjusted because of me. But obviously, not everybody agrees.

CHARLOTTE's experience was quite different:

I adopted Tanya from El Salvador when I was thirty-nine. It's very interesting, because my mother was thirty-nine when she had me. It's just amazing the way things turn out. I was raised by a single mother; my parents were divorced when I was an infant. There was nothing in my life that would ever have told me that I would reproduce my family constellation, even in a healthy way, which I think I have done. I thought I could never be a single parent of a single child. To me that would have been to repeat my mother's pattern and become my depressed, hostile, angry mother.

I always thought that I had to be married and have several children, and that, if I wasn't married by the time I was thirty-five, I had better adjust to the fact that I wouldn't get married and have kids. One of the most freeing experiences I ever had was when I suddenly realized that there was another way to have kids, because it seemed clear that things were not going to work out in the conventional way for me. I just didn't ever know what it was like to live with a man, as I had never lived with one in my home from the time I was two-and-a-half. I guess I just had no idea what it was like to make the compromises. Men turned out to be rather foreign to me; they weren't natural to me. There were plenty of opportunities— there was one person who was a real opportunity missed—but they never seemed to work out.

More than not having a father at home, I think it was my mother's inability to find a normal father substitute for me. Of course, it's important to have a father, but it's important for a child to have a man in his or her life. I saw my father twice a year, at most. I have made sure that Tanya has a man in her life; my friend's husband has made a commitment to be there for her.

Being a single mother is like second nature to me, because I was raised by a single mother. I know what it is to do everything, and I feel absolutely competent. The hardest part is the finances. It's very hard to have no other income. Also, there's not another person in your life who cares as much about this child as you do.

I knew I wanted a girl and a healthy baby. I didn't care about the race; Tanya's brown and I am white. She looks Hispanic, and I consider her transcultural. I am raising her as a Methodist, but I really want her to know about her culture, also.

The first couple of weeks after I brought her home people

would ask, "Is this your kid?" and I would say, "Yes, she's my girl!" People say to me, "She must look like her father," and I don't say anything. Now, when I see other mothers whose kids look different from them, I bite my tongue. I know this person has no reason to give me her personal data. We look different, but she is my child, and I have the same feelings as biological mothers I talk to.

I grew up as an only child, which I didn't like, and I would love Tanya to have a sibling. I think she will have a father some day, that I will get married. But if I don't, it's OK. I think getting married was something that was much more important in the past. The partner was important because, on some level, he meant that I could have a family—because you can always have a partner, but as a woman, you cannot always have a family. Your biological clock is ticking. It was a relief for me to know that my having a family, which means kids, was not tied to making a good match with a man. Maybe even a child was really what I wanted. Maybe I want a partner, maybe I don't.

KAREN adopted her daughter, now two, from Texas. A slim, blond woman, with pretty, if somewhat pinched, features, Karen is a primary-school teacher:

I applied to Texas because the birth mother has only two days to change her mind there. That's why Texas is so popular. Every state has a different requirement. In New York, it is forty-five days. According to Texas law, they will not pair you up until the birth mother has signed the relinquishing papers. They also require all adoptions to be completed through an agency, which most states don't do.

The good thing about going through an agency is that all births are registered in a central registry. The agency gives the description, but not the name. If the birth mother allows the information to be released, and if Susan agrees to have her birth information released, if one of them does a search, they will be able to find each other.

Every agency will tell you that they accept singles because, legally, they have to, but you may be at the bottom of the list. I heard about his agency that was very open to singles adopting. They told me they could get me a baby within nine months to a year. A lot of agencies require seven to eight thousand dollars right up front, but this one didn't require money until you were much further down the road.

It was about a year after I had registered with them and I remember calling them up one day. And, guess what, they had just pulled my file and asked me if I was interested in a baby. Here I was, sitting with a colleague, my mouth dropping open, and I was saying, "I can't believe this is happening!" The next week I was on a plane to collect my baby. I picked her up at the airport. All I had to do was to sign the papers; they had formula and a diaper bag with everything in it for one day.

My mother was here for two weeks, and she was very helpful. But I remember the first time I was alone in the apartment with this newborn. I got really scared; I was terrified. I managed to change her diaper. It made me realize that I had the resources within me, that I really have dealt with children for a long time, and that my impulses with kids are very good.

Karen, forty-one, is one of two siblings and grew up in a suburb of Cleveland:

My family couldn't have been more traditional. My mother never worked, and my father was a physicist. We presented a picture of the perfect family. It was important for my parents to have children who were the best family in the community. But I can't remember a time when I felt there weren't underlying tensions between them. My mother would never admit it, but she was probably very angry. Mother didn't really enjoy children that much, and it's hard to imagine that she enjoyed me and my brother.

I think that all this played somehow into the decision to become a single parent. I never really believed in marriage. I often envisioned myself having a child, but marriage didn't seem like a necessary prerequisite. I thought that I would get married, and I very rarely didn't have a boyfriend, but they weren't men who had any intention of getting married. If my goal was to stay unmarried, I picked very well. I have always had a lot of friends, both men and women, and have been very sociable. But the myth of perfection in my family was such a total farce that I didn't want to run the risk of having that experience myself.

I always knew I wanted to have children. I've been involved with children since I was a kid myself. I used to be a candystriper in the pediatric ward of a hospital. I had a cousin who had adopted, and all of a sudden, I thought I could do that. I was about thirty-eight when I started to think about it seriously.

My father's response really surprised me. He turned to me and said, "Well, I can understand how you'd want a child." But my mother went absolutely white. She was beyond tears; she didn't know what to say. She wouldn't look me in the eye. Finally, I asked her what was troubling her so much, and she said she had never known a single parent before! Even though I knew it was much deeper than that, I could get a handle on that. She got more and more used to it, but she wouldn't allow herself to think of a biracial child. I think it's a tremendous relief to her that Susie's skin is white, also that I had her converted and joined a synagogue. I was always very clear that I would raise her as a Jewish child.

I don't know if it was biological, but I knew that I had to have a child; I yearned for one. I don't think I ever really questioned whether I could raise a child alone. I was happy before, but it's a different kind of happiness. She's filled a huge hole—I didn't even really know how big it was. It's been an extraordinary change. She's almost two now; she goes to a day care provider during the day. The worst part for me is that I am chronically fatigued.

Unlike other single adoptive parents interviewed here, Karen is involved in an ongoing relationship, but with a married man:

I don't consider myself single, yet I don't consider myself married. In Susie's life, I am very much a single parent, and I think I do very well with her alone. Joe is very much involved in providing me with emotional support and closeness. I don't know if I would have had the guts or felt I could do it without that support. They do have a relationship, and I hope that she will never be confused about Joe's not being her father. When she's old enough to understand, I plan to tell her that he's my lover, because that's what he is.

I ask Karen what her aspirations are for Susie:

I hope she will be as happy at age forty as I have been. I hope there are as many people close to her as there are to me. I imagine her not wanting to talk to me or spend time with me when she's a teenager, and that's very painful for me. When there's one parent and one child, it's pretty intense, which creates potential problems if you don't do something to prevent them.

I knew that I had to have a child. I very much hope that she has children. I don't know whether I hope that she gets married or not. I've not given her much of a role model for marriage.

ADOPTING AN OLDER CHILD

SYLVIA is in her mid-forties and grew up in a small midwestern town, the middle of three children of a working-class family. She is a mathematics teacher at a parochial school, and her short, curly hair, horn-rimmed glasses, and aquiline features give her a somewhat boyish appearance:

My mother and father had a stormy marriage. I think it's

the reason why none of their children is married. When I was much younger, I assumed I would be married, but for some reason, I always thought I would adopt children. My son is the only grandchild. Growing up in a house where the parents were always fighting led us not to see marriage as too positive. Three out of three are pretty good odds, I was always close to my mother, but I haven't been very close to my father.

I was approaching thirty and saw that marriage wasn't happening. Somehow, I would start looking for flaws, and after a while, I think men would pick up that something was wrong, that I was holding back. As a teacher, I come in contact with kids a lot, and I found myself kind of falling in love with certain kids, and at the end of the year, they graduated.

I remember many years ago reading an article in *Ms.* magazine about single women who had adopted. Reading this article made me realize this was possible. I was concerned about going through pregnancy physically, and as I worked with elementary-school kids, I felt comfortable with that age. I leaned toward a boy because my favorite students were always boys. Finally, I said to myself, "I will go to an adoption agency," but I didn't tell anyone until I was ready to adopt.

The agency was pushing foster care, but I couldn't take the chance of loving a child and losing a child. And then I met a person who has contacts in Paraguay. I thought I could accept a child who was nonwhite, a Spanish or a biracial child. I found out about Ernest when he was four. He was living with his biological mother and other siblings; it was basically a matter of poverty. A certain price was quoted, and then it turned out that he was six, so they lowered it. When I was told his age, I had to make a decision, because I had every right to say, "Forget it." I was shown a picture of him, and I finally said, "This kid is available. Let's pursue it."

Once I accepted him in name, I felt as if I was walking closer and closer to the edge of a cliff. I said to myself, "I cannot stop myself. I have to go over the cliff." But still, I was very anxious; it was a life-changing situation. I kept looking at children who were his age, and some of them were really big. So in my mind, I was saying, "Stay little, so I have a few months with you to hug and cuddle and stuff."

When I finally told my mother, she said "How come you want to do something that might ruin your whole life?" But surprisingly, my father, who I normally didn't see eye-to-eye with, seemed much more understanding.

I gave the facilitator a deposit and was able to get more pictures and ask her some questions. I got a medical report on him and was assured he was normal and bright. I also had to go to a psychologist, and the report had to be translated and sent to Paraguay.

By the time he came here, he was seven. My mother and father and I went to the airport to pick him up. I was pacing; I was a wreck. I had taken two weeks off work. I remember his hair being very dull, from malnutrition. He didn't speak English, but I spoke a little Spanish. He was very placid; he was in shock for a couple of days. The first few days, he was very quiet. He wouldn't say anything, even if I asked him if he was hungry. I just had to put the food in front of him, and then he would eat.

He'd never been to school. That was a bit of a disaster for a while, and don't ask about child care; that was a whole other story! If I hadn't had my parents to give me some respite, I don't know how I would have managed. But after six months, he was speaking English, and now he's in the fourth grade and about on grade level. There were times when he hated English and would hold his ears and say it was ugly. Other times, he held his ears when he heard Spanish.

Most of the people I see now on a regular basis are other single adoptive parents. I feel that is good for my son. We are an unusual family, but not in our social group, and we know a lot of other children from Paraguay. My son is very outgoing, and he's made me more friends. Socially, it's been great because I was not a person who went out a lot.

He loves Paraguay and calls it "my country." I used to give Ernest pictures, and he would look at them all the time. Now he doesn't look so much. It took him a year before he would call me "Mom." It was very hard for me to wait that year. I am his mother until he thinks about Paraguay. Yet people tell me he is always talking bout me, and he's so proud of me.

This Christmas, I took Ernest to pick out a Spanish Christmas card for his mother and showed him which pictures I was sending her. Up until this point, I had not done that. He talked about it; I think he feels that she gave him up. She did contact the facilitator once and said she was so glad to know my son was doing well.

In his daily life, definitely I am his mom, and I think he loves me and that we are both happy. At home, he's very needy because of the situation he's been through, and he's very kissy and huggy, probably more than most boys of his age. I guess what's hard is he wasn't here as a baby; it's certainly much sooner that he's going to be out and independent. Now, when he's with his friends, he doesn't want me around. He has to be Mr. Macho and stuff, and I understand, but it's sort of hard.

He had not been given any kind of religious education, and I am a practicing Protestant in a very low-key manner, which he has been exposed to. There was a point recently when we discussed the fact that he would have to choose, and he said, "What if I choose to be a Catholic?" I said, "It's OK. It's your choice. You're my son, and I still love you." He once said to me, "I think I love my other family better than my current family." I said, "I don't know if you have to love either family better. Why can't you just love both families?" and he seemed to think that was OK.

I do have some fear that, when he grows up, he might want to go back to Paraguay, but I don't want him to feel bad about himself or feel bad about his country. Some day, I will give him a trip there, but I can't do it just yet. Maybe it's too soon for me.

There are times when it has been really, really hard, but I think it's the best thing I ever did. Even if he weren't my son, I honestly think he's a wonderful child. He's very bright and charming, and I would do it all over again.

STEVEN recently finalized the adoption of his two sons, now eleven and twelve, whom he got from Brazil two years ago:

They were very wild when they first came, and very greedy. During the first week, I was saying to myself, "I hope I have not made the greatest mistake of my life." They were off the wall because there was no structure, and then school clicked in and everything began to calm down. They told me much later that they immediately got a very strong positive feel for me, but they had nothing to lose.

They took to living here like ducks to water. They hated Brazil because of how they had lived their lives there. They talk somewhat fondly of their father but have nothing good to say about their mother, who hurt them. I wanted to give them a positive impression of Brazilian people, and I have Brazilian ladies to take care of them. If they go through life thinking Brazil is a bad place, they will transfer that to some extent to themselves.

At the beginning, I was pretty concerned about the older boy. They have to have lots of bad stuff inside them, and maybe some day it will come out. I always keep my eye out for something occurring that might trigger that, but so far, they have adjusted well.

Their school situation has been a bit harder to adjust to but they are on grade level, and according to their reports, they seem pretty normal kids. They're very motivated and want to please. It does come out occasionally that they are very grateful, but most often they are just ordinary kids on the block.

Steven proudly tells me how each boy recently won a basketball trophy:

I've always loved children, and there was never a question that I would have children. I waited until I was economically in a situation where I could adopt and provide children with what they should have. I am quite comfortable with my decision to be single. I have a modest social life, and I have had girlfriends at various times in my life. I have enjoyed the dating and the intimacy, but I have not met any woman that I actually wanted to live with. To me, personally, it's not something that I'm particularly interested in. Which doesn't mean that, if someone came around and really knocked me over, I would have some sort of great objection.

Life experiences have shown me that people are just built differently. During one period, I was wondering if something was wrong with me, and I had to ask myself, "Are you unhappy?" and I wasn't. I'm also convinced that, unless you really want to live with someone, it has to be something that comes from within you, and that just never happened with me.

I have had very positive role models, in both my parents and my siblings. I come from a large family. My father is very much a family man, and my mother always seemed to enjoy what she did. She always put her children first. My parents and my family definitely would be much happier if I did get married. My mother was particularly unthrilled with the idea of my adopting. Both of them were, because the net result is that you're not such a hot prospect. My father one time said to me, "Why don't you do this more conventionally, get married and have kids?" I was very concerned that my family would be accepting of the boys. Personally, I don't care about color at all, but I had to cut out kids who were really dark-skinned. I thought it wise to adopt a boy, and I also definitely did not want an infant.

I have two wonderful kids and I look forward to every

part of my job as a parent. The worst thing is being stretched trying to balance my profession with being a father, but I think I can serve both of those roles pretty well. At the beginning, the most helpful thing was that my youngest sister came daily for the first six months. But I really don't think there's much that a woman can do that I can't do. It doesn't make any difference if the child is your own biologically or not. I also think there are women who are as well equipped to be both mother and father.

In some ways my life has not changed at all. In other ways, my life fundamentally revolves around the children and work. I carve out time for me, because if I don't do that, I'm not going to be as good a parent. The things that I enjoy in my private life, I still manage to maintain in a scaled-back form. I make time in the evening to call friends and chew the fat, and I read an enormous amount. On the other hand, I enjoy taking my kids to Little League; I very much enjoy that part of raising them. So I've managed to balance it.

I think most kids are eager to see single fathers get married, and mine have tangentially mentioned it. I haven't dated much since I have had them, and I don't really have single women friends. Most of the women I am friendly with are married to my friends.

People think that I am a savior, but it's not like that—you really have to want to do this. It also helps to have a lot of money. In a way, I have it much easier than having a former spouse out there, with all the pressures and divided loyalties. My kids are mine, and it makes life a lot simpler.

I would like to adopt again, but not soon. They are not keen on the idea, so I will probably wait three to five years down the road. I hope they are able to reach their aspirations, given the best education available, and a nice life. My basic hopes have already been fulfilled, which are having two nice kids. I don't care what they do, as long as they are happy.

ADOPTING INTERRACIALLY

TRUDY, *the mother of two-year-old Brian, whom she adopted as a boarder baby, has two married siblings, both of whom have children:*

My parents had a wonderful marriage and got along well. My father was a businessman, and my mother worked in an office. I was always very close to them.

I never had the desire to have a child. I never found infants cute and adorable until I was in my forties. Then I had a relationship with a man who had partial custody of his son, who was three. I was around that child quite a bit, which was a new experience for me, and I realized children aren't half bad. I enjoyed it; it was fun. I think also as I got older, I developed more patience and didn't see children as a nuisance.

This was the first time that I ever thought I might get married. Bottom line, intimate relationships have always made me feel smothered. I had a lot of losses when I was young, several close relatives dying, and in my family once someone was dead, you didn't talk about them. I also think my mother was quite depressed after her father died, which also happened when I was very young.

This was the first really solid relationship I had had. I've always had an independent life and have lots of friends, but my relationships with men have never been that great; they never lasted that long. I'd have relationships, but it was never consistent, and I would sometimes go for long periods without seeing anyone. I still had difficulties with Nick, but he was a wonderful person and I felt very secure. Looking back, I see it as an integral part of my getting to the point where I could have this intimate relationship with a child, because nothing is as intimate as that.

The relationship finally broke up; he left me. Separation has always been an issue for me, but the fact that I was able to survive it, because it was so painful for me, made me feel stronger. I was a mess for a year, but I came out of it functioning better than I had ever functioned before.

Adoption always appealed to me and was my first choice once I decided to bring a child into my life. It's the most extraordinary thing I have ever done; it has changed my life on so many levels and in so many ways. I was originally going to go through a foreign source, but that didn't work out. Then someone suggested taking a boarder baby to test out whether I really wanted a child. I took a boarder baby in a three-month program, and I was able to see what it was like having a baby in my life, and it was nice.

One change is that they allow working parents to adopt now. Years ago you couldn't do that. I was working full time when I got Brian. He was ten days old, and I had to get a baby-sitter. He's been with the same woman now almost since birth, and I would like him to stay there for another year. It's family day care in a house, and she has a license. It's very nice. There are cooking smells when he goes there.

At first it was very scary. I don't bond instantly, so it took me a while. I'm not the type of person who sees a baby and falls in love with him and says, "I can't live my life without this baby." The law is that the birth mother has thirty days to renege if it's an agency, forty-five if it's an independent adoption. It offers you some breathing space, which, for me, was good. Eventually, I became very attached to Brian. I had to deal with the interracial issue, too.

So far it's been fine, but I think it gets harder for children as they get older. I anticipate that he's going to have more difficulty having an older mother than having a white mother. I have a feeling he might become more self-conscious about that than anything else. I am not in contact with the birth mother, but I have information about where she lives. One of the nice things about adopting through the child welfare system is that there is a central registry. When he gets older, he can put his name into the registry, and, if they are both looking for each other, that information will be available to them and they can find each other.

Male role models are on my mind, and there are men in his life. I think that's important, but I don't think it's everything; it didn't stop me from adopting. After all, there are so many one-parent families. My fantasy is that I will meet a person of color and get married, and Brian will have a black daddy. That would solve a lot of problems. If I happen to meet someone, I think it will probably be a pretty stable and maybe permanent thing, but it's not a primary concern of mine. Sometimes, I think, "Should I go the rest of my life without sex?" and I don't think that's so good. Issues of relationships do impinge, depending on how painful they are. Right now, it's not painful, but when he's a teenager and going through his own sexual issues, I think it would be better if I had my own sex life. When he's going off and being independent and having his fun, I don't want to feel that I missed out. I think it will be fine, but I don't want to have that little envious tug in terms of his sexuality. But if I missed out, it wouldn't be because of him; it would be because of myself.

I think that when you are older maybe there's less of an empty-nest syndrome because maybe at that point it might be nice to have a little freedom. When you are forty, you are still in the middle of your life, and you want a career. Empty-nest syndrome might not be such a big deal if you're also not going through a midlife crisis.

Having Brian has affected my life in every which way. I have more friends than I ever had. I am a member of a single-parent group, and we all have so much in common. I consider myself single and postsingle, because it's like not being single anymore. I still have pre-Brian friends, but I tend to socialize now more with my other friends, because I'm not as free to go out as I used to be. I was tired of going to dinners and to shows and to movies and theaters and museums, even though I loved them; I had had enough. When people talk about sacrifice, all I can say is that the quality of my life has improved enormously. It is the most wonderful thing, the best. I think I am a reasonably good parent, and that's a nice feeling, having a relationship with this child and watching him develop. My life is fuller and I feel less lonely.

I have such a positive attitude about adoption that I am hoping that will be communicated in my handling of Brian. I know that there will be hard times ahead, and that's OK. Whatever he goes through, I will try to be there for him. I think when I decided to adopt a black child, I also decided that life doesn't have to be easy, not that I want to wear a hair shirt, but that it could be a challenge and it would be fine.

RHODA *is a large-framed, handsome-looking woman with shoulder-length curly blond hair. Aged forty-four, she works as a kindergarten teacher:*

I come from a middle-class, pretty traditional family. I have two brothers. We had a large extended family and there were always a lot of people around. I feel I have very good memories, but my parents didn't have the greatest relationship. My father used to flare up and then stop talking, sometimes for days at a time. It was very frightening. My mother kind of accepted it, and I would always try to be the peacemaker. When I got older, they had a better relationship; it was more loving.

I adopted an older child because I felt I couldn't handle an infant by myself. Also I did not have the strong need to do the baby bit. My relationships with men had been very unsatisfying. It just seemed that I was picking the wrong people. I did date someone for eight years who was not the best kind of person for me. Guys were very interested, but if they were too available, somehow I would lose it. Talk about regrets! But if I had to do it over again, it might come to the same thing. I think it had to do with feelings about myself, that if someone liked me so much, he couldn't be that terrific. But then I never heard my parents say, "I am proud of you," or "You are successful." It was always the "but" and "do more."

I didn't give up the idea of getting married, and I wanted a nuclear family very, very badly. I felt this need to nurture. I had a lot of friends who had recently been divorced and were raising children by themselves. They were really alone, and from my perspective, they seemed to be doing nicely. I think that was a big influence. I had been thinking about it a long time; it was a long process. I guess I was feeling very lonely. It also seemed easier in a sense than a guy, because the men that I liked were very difficult.

There were very few single people who adopted in the early eighties. Now it is completely different and has become much easier. It's amazing! You join a group, and you feel as if everybody in the world is doing the same thing. I heard about an adoption lawyer through LAPA (Latin American Parents' Association). He ran a nursery in Costa Rica and sent me pictures. From the time I first contacted him to the time I got Felice took about ten months. He gave out about a hundred babies that year, and then it just stopped and he disappeared.

I went down by myself and stayed in the hotel with Felice for five days. She was just four at the time; now she's almost twelve. She did not speak English, but we had a translator. It was kind of scary. I was a little surprised because she was darker-skinned than the pictures showed, so the first day, it was very difficult for me. I was very angry at the lawyer. I was even thinking of just dropping it and maybe starting over. I started thinking about all the difficulties, how this was going to affect lots of things, my relationships with my family, friends, school. It's one thing knowing that a child is adopted, and another having such a difference in skin color where it can be so identified. I was torn about having a whole new life; there was one very strong piece in this that I had not anticipated. She was staying with me in the hotel, and I did not understand how frightened she must have been. By the second day, something just happened, and she was my child.

Her racial background has had a very strong impact on her relationships with people. My family have been very accepting and supportive, but it did make a difference in school. The Hispanic kids are the ones that come over to her, and she is not that friendly with the white kids. Kids pick their own, and this is what she feels comfortable with. They are basically OK kids, but they have different values; there aren't any Hispanic kids who are middle-class. At times, I get annoyed. It's like my attitude is "She has a choice, and why is she picking this when she could pick that?"

I would like her to look like me; I would like us to look closer together. I still feel uncomfortable about it because we are close, and there has been a bonding, and I look at her, and she is so different. It just hits me. I want her to be of me, mine, at least to look like me, but it's such a stark difference.

The best part is such a feeling of fulfillment, this connection with another person. It's a joy, things that happen at different moments that are so satisfying, just watching her grow and be happy. Felice is so wonderful. I feel that I have grown so much as a person. You reach a certain point where it can't be "me, me, me" all the time. I see my single friends, and they are still into "me, me, me." I think you just get something by taking care of another person.

When things get very rough I think, "What do I need a child for," but it's kind of fleeting; it doesn't stay very long. It goes without saying that money is a big issue. She very much wanted a brother or sister, and if I were more financially able, I certainly would have done it. The biggest problem is always feeling that if an emergency arises, I am alone. I have friends, but I have this general feeling of being vulnerable. I need someone to talk to, to run things by, to have her pick up values from. That's important, children usually learn by hearing adults talking to each other. I feel she doesn't know me really well. She hears me talking to a child, not to an intimate.

She always went to men and formed relationships quickly with them. She wants a father; she would say the family is incomplete. When we are walking down the street and see a family—say, a father carrying a child on his shoulders—she will stop in her tracks and start staring at them. I think assimilation and identity will be very big in years to come. But I think for Felice, if she came from an intact family or had a sibling, our relationship would be less intense, and the other things—the adoption, skin color—would not be much of an issue.

The fact is that I was so emotionally drained from men. I was so thrilled to be out from the scene with them, I just couldn't deal with them. On a Saturday night, I was just as pleased to spend my time with other women who felt the same as I did. But now I feel I am at a new chapter. Now Felice is getting older, I would be interested in starting to date again.

ADOPTING A HANDICAPPED CHILD

BERNICE, a mild-mannered, heavyset woman of forty-two, wearing glasses and a friendly smile, initially took Arthur in as a foster child shortly after he was born. Arthur was born addicted to crack:

I decided that I wanted to have a child, and there were all these boarder babies for whom they were searching for foster care. I was working as a social worker at a day care center at the time, and all the staff had been fingerprinted, so we were a ripe population to ask. I thought about it for a long time, and I thought, "The worst that can happen is that the child will go back to its biological parent, and I'll have some better idea about how I feel about being a single parent." There was that train of thought that adopting a child is very self-indulgent, but I was looking for a child who needed me.

I had a foster child for two weeks. It was very intense and terrifying. I had no idea what it was going to be like. He was a crack baby, also. Nobody knew anything about crack then. Many of the boarder babies have AIDS or are addicted to crack. Babies can be HIV positive, and after eighteen months, they can test negative, but it is not always the case. With crack babies, the crack goes out of their system after three months, but they don't really know what the residual effects are.

Bernice grew up in a traditional family in the Midwest and has one younger sister who is married and has two children. Both her parents are teachers:

My parents were somewhat perfectionist. They were screamers. They fought a fair amount, but there were a lot of good times, too. I thought I would get married. I had a couple of relationships, but I never really met anybody where we got that far. It was very hard for my parents at first when I adopted Arthur. There was as much controversy about his being black as about my being single. But they really love me a lot, and they respect my decisions. They've done a lot of changing, but it was hard for them. It still is.

I took Arthur thinking that I was doing a good deed, and that maybe I'd adopt him. The first three months were difficult. I didn't have any backup from the agency. I was left totally to my own devices. In the beginning, he was really fussy and very colicky. He had a lot of high fevers and seemed prone to illnesses. I think that probably had something to do with the crack. There are two reactions to crack; one is lethargy and the other is agitation. Arthur was more agitated. Also, his skin was very sensitive to touch, and he was easily overstimulated. He still has a very low frustration tolerance. He's not hyperactive, but there's a flurry of activity most of the time.

The mother is still on crack. At one point, she wanted him back, and that was a very difficult time for both of us. I don't think I would ever have wanted to give him up after I got him, even though it did take a long time to get used to. You get a reimbursement for a foster child; I still get a subsidy. The money made it possible; I don't think I could have done it otherwise. It also made be able to be home with him more, rather than paying baby-sitters.

Arthur has a lot of separation anxieties. He was in the hospital for the first month of his life, and maybe the anxieties come from that. I think I have really been able to have an effect on the belligerence and low frustration tolerance and overstimulation. The difficulties push people's buttons. It took me a long time to realize that, and I had to work very hard on my reactions to his outbursts. My theory is that crack is so powerful maybe it fires the nerves. He seems bigger than life. He's so much of everything that other children seem bland to me. His teacher adores him. She says he's a real leader. Because I have a lot of contacts, I was able to find the best nursery school for him.

He's changed so much. The belligerence and low frustration are much less. People often think I am the foster parent or guardian. I felt a bit show-offy at first. It was fun having this little baby and people looking. But I would hear obnoxious comments like "You like to baby-sit?" and it was very annoying. I am concerned about how he will feel, and I can definitely see that explaining is not going to be so easy. The adoption is more obvious, and one of these days, he's going to realize it, and then it's going to be a whole other thing. The other day, Arthur turned to me and said, "Mommy, I wish you were brown." He also needs a male figure. He asks for a daddy a lot and always goes to men. I am hoping to find someone for him, maybe a big brother.

I asked Bernice what it was like raising Arthur alone:

It's just harder, but there are some rewards. I don't have to fight with anybody, but I also don't get any feedback. It's just more complicated, but I don't think it's that much different. What's really amazing is how all the feelings and experiences I have are really the same as those of any other parent, biological or adoptive.

I really believe that, for the most part, the difficulties with crack can be overcome. If everybody said no to this, then all of these children would be in hospitals and other kinds of settings that are less beneficial. If I had known then what he is like now, I would not have been so afraid. I believe that the environment can have an enormous effect and that many of these children can be adopted. The rewards of having a happy child who is excited about discovering things, and is so bright, and finds so many new ways to get what he wants are more than I can say. It was a lot of hard work for me, and I had to grow up a lot, but I got and get an enormous amount out of it, reaching inside and finding patience and extra resources. It's very enriching to me, and I feel a lot wiser.

MARGARET, the mother of sixteen-year-old Janice, who is retarded, and five-month-old Jason, who has Down syndrome, was the youngest of five children:

My father was a forceful man who drank on weekends. My parents stayed together, but I'm not sure they always wanted to. My mother was a martyr: She had to stay for the sake of the children. Even though their marriage improved as they became older, I think the earlier trouble contributed a lot to my not marrying.

Even so, I grew up with the thought that I would be married. My brother's marriage was my model. He was fourteen years older than I, and when his marriage dissolved after twenty-three years, it was earth-shaking for me. This was the ideal marriage, and at that point, I realized it was not the most important thing for me to be married, that it was a means to an end, that what I wanted most was a child.

I was dating a doctor while I was in nursing school and was going to marry him. This was the marriage that should have been, but my parents wouldn't accept him because he was Catholic. I was in another relationship for about three years after that, and there were other casual relationships. I am a person who keeps very close friends. I have had one of my friends since I was ten years old.

I always wanted to be a nurse. I was working in a hospital with children who were handicapped, and there was one child who was "my baby." I always had him every time he came into the hospital. There were handicapped kids all over the place who were in intermediate-care facilities when they didn't need to be. But there were no homes for them. This was the baby who made me realize that I did not need a husband to have a child. I had the time, and I had the need to satisfy something, and these kids had a need that I could fulfill. They needed me and I needed them, because there was something missing in my life, an extension of my love, my caring. I didn't see this in terms of a relationship, because that was a sharing, not an extension.

It took me three years to get a child, which was unbelievably fast in those days. I adopted Janice when she was seven. No one even knew that she was available, even though she had supposedly been free for adoption for three-and-a-half years. The agency was doing nothing to get her adopted. They were really bad. They allowed her to come into my home for five days, and they never supervised her visit; they never brought her to my house, they never saw my house. I could have been Jack the Ripper for all they knew!

My mother loved Janice very much, but Janice's hyperactivity drove her crazy. Janice was severely handicapped and almost nonverbal when I got her. During those first few months, my mother practically lived with us. That was my backup and support, and we were constantly losing baby-sitters. I got a stipend for Janice, but it still wasn't easy. The positives are the accomplishments she has made and knowing that they are there because of things that I have done for her.

I knew that bringing this child into my life would mean a loss. But there was nothing in my life that was missing at that point that I wanted to do so badly that, for the next fifteen to twenty years, I couldn't set aside to meet the needs of that child. She changed my life a lot. I knew that people would not accept this child, but those people who could not accept her for who she was, I did not need in my life. My friends said, "You're not available, you're always running home to Janice," and my best friend didn't speak to me.

I didn't know how to balance her and a relationship of any kind, so it was easier not to have a relationship. There's a lot less pressure being alone. There's a lot more for the kids. Now that I have the kids, I can waiver on that—now that I have successfully done the mothering of my daughter, who, at twenty-one, will be leaving me to go on to adult life. When she is twenty-one, she will go into some kind of group setting and will, I hope, be able to do something in an entry-level position. I know now that a marriage provides that other person, that other pair of hands. But you have to have the right husband, especially with handicapped kids; they take a lot of time. There's more flexibility in single parenting, unless you have the right marriage. I know there are marriages like that, but they are not necessarily in my immediate surroundings.

Male role models are very important. We have lots of friends and a brother-in-law who is marvelous with Janice, and we are actively involved in the church. There are significant males in her life.

I wanted three kids, and it wasn't easy, even to get a second child. Janice had some friends who have Down syndrome. I was turned off by it at first, but a lot more is being done for these children now. So when I got the call for Jason, I said I'd take him. He has a teacher who comes to the house twice a week, and he goes out to school once a week for speech. When he's tired, his tongue hangs out and his eyes focus inward.

My mother said parenting is not something that everybody should do, and I really believe it. Whether you can be a parent biologically or not, there are some who shouldn't be parents. I will be sixty-five when Jason leaves the nest. Then I'll sit back and put up my feet and relax because I will have done my job. I will have done what I wanted to do: raise these kids.

SUMMARY

The motivations for parenthood in singles who adopt appear very similar to those of single biological parents, even though in some instances more altruism seems to prevail. Perhaps, for this reason, society is more favorably disposed toward single adoptions than toward single pregnancies. Certainly, the actual experience of adopting may be infinitely more complex. One might say that this method of becoming a parent is at times as painful as childbirth.

The reasons for wanting children tap into a complex array of emotions. Having children enables us to deal with our own issues of mortality. It is likely that people choosing to adopt do not have as strong a need as others to see themselves genetically replicated. Only one parent really spoke of wanting to have a love child to be shared with a partner, and when that no longer seemed feasible, she did not feel the need to see her genes replicated. For many the wish for a child was more important than the desire for a partner.

One mother said that single parents often discuss whether they are prepared to share their child with another person. Another mother, who described having wanted to adopt ever since she was twelve years old, wondered how much this desire had been related to an unhappy childhood filled with thoughts of wanting to have been adopted herself. Although I am not suggesting that the desire to adopt is necessarily a reaction to wishing that oneself had been adopted, it may be that Freud's family romance fantasy is particularly strong in people who wanted to adopt from an early age.

Whatever the reasons for choosing to adopt, the question must still be asked: How does the experience of adopted children growing up with a single parent compare with the experience of those growing up in a two-parent family?

One mother described her own experience:

I grew up with such a traditional family: mother, father, and three children. Even though we knew that it was a dysfunctional family, the way it was looked at by the community, it seemed all OK. But I'm sure that we had many more problems in coping with life than my child will have. I know she is getting more in terms of consistent and child-centered interaction with a mother than I ever got with two parents.

Chapter 5

Single Parents by Divorce

*For the first time in our history, two
people entering marriage are just as likely
to be parted by divorce as by death.*

Lenore J. Weitzman[1]

Although most Americans continue to marry, the number of couples getting divorced has gone up exponentially in recent decades. These figures started to climb in 1963, reaching an all-time high in 1979. In that year, 1.21 million marriages, or more than 2 marriages in 100, were terminated by divorce.[2] This proportion constituted twice as many than at the peak of the baby boom years, when divorce affected fewer than 1 in 100.[3]

Recent statistics indicate that 10.1 percent, or 14 million, of *all* ever-married Americans alive today have been divorced, at least once. This means that anyone getting married today has only a 50-50 chance of staying married "until death do us part."[4]

Although people in the past were more likely to stay in an unsatisfying marriage "for the sake of the children," this no longer appears to be the case. During the 1980s, approximately 61 percent of all households with dependent children included both biological mother and biological father, 24 percent were headed by single parents, 12 percent were "blended" or remarried families, and the remaining 3 percent consisted of other combinations.[5]

Divorce rates started to plateau in the 1980s and have been going down slightly each year since 1987. However, this shift is not enough to warrant changes in current predictions, which hypothesize that about half of all marriages that have taken place in the last couple of decades will eventually end in divorce.[6] This means that about half of all children born in those marriages will spend some time before their sixteenth birthday living in a one-parent family.[7]

Even though so many marriages seem doomed to failure, once people have experienced marriage, most wish to return to the conjugal state once, or even twice. Even though the divorce rate for remarriages is slightly higher than for the first time around, one out of every three Americans marrying today is doing so for at least the second time.[8]

Although a large proportion of divorced people are anxious to remarry, or certainly express the desire to do so, by no means all are so eager to return to "marital bliss." The following are some of the comments from divorcees eschewing marriage:

> I definitely didn't want to get remarried. I felt a huge commitment to my kids, and I thought that really would interfere with another relationship.

> If someone else came in, it would ruin it. I wouldn't want it, and my child wouldn't want it.

> Between working and trying to be a good mother, there isn't time and energy for much else.

> I decided that being married and getting divorced were basically financial transactions. When the marriage ended, it was all about money and a redistribution of property. I decided that I'd had the experience of being married and I didn't need to be married again.

> I don't really like the idea of being married, being closed in.

> That old song "Don't Fence Me In" expresses my feelings exactly.

> I am frightened of making a mistake again. I don't trust my judgment enough.

> I have four cats. I love being alone. I spend weekends alone by choice.

Not wanting to marry again clearly does not necessarily exclude the wish to be in a romantic relationship. Many of those interviewed had experienced at least one relatively long-term relationship after divorce, and in some cases, living with a partner in a marriage-like state. What was apparent in some cases was a wish to avoid the legality of marriage or the commitment to another adult:

> Rob is still married to his wife, so there's no pressure for me to marry him. Because I don't want to ever feel trapped into something that I can't get out of—that's the way it was in my marriage.

> I could have a loving relationship with somebody. It's not necessary to be married, except that it's a protection for the children.

> I like being with my companion, and we really enjoy each other, but I like having my own space. I like having my own apartment. I like having those nights of the week when I am alone. You do get used to that.

> There's still this vulnerability to rejection. But I think, well, not yet. Maybe we'll get married later—we'll see.

> When you live alone, there are certain things that you want done a certain way. It might change, but right now, I really like the way things are.

> I know if something happens, there'll be no messy legal entanglement.

Clearly, there are many reasons for people choosing to

remain divorced. Some are positive, like enjoying a sense of independence or pleasure in one's own company. Others suggest underlying anxieties, such as the fear of repeating past mistakes or reexperiencing old losses. Many of the people interviewed felt that remarriage, or the introduction of another adult relationship into their lives, would be detrimental to their children as it might interfere with their role as parents.

Before we are introduced further to these parents, we are going to take a brief look at the history of divorce in the United States.

HISTORY OF DIVORCE

American divorce laws have early ties to English common law, which, itself, was very much influenced by the Church. Marriage was viewed as a sacrament, a holy union between a man and a woman, to be ended only by death. Divorce was, accordingly, seen as an unacceptable violation of the sacrament. The State was expected to conform to the Church's teachings and to protect marriage by restricting access to divorce. As a result, legal divorce in the modern sense did not exist in England until the mid-1800s. The only way to obtain a divorce was through a special act of Parliament, which was passed in the late seventeenth century and permitted divorce only on the grounds of adultery. Although it was still possible to get a legal separation *a mensa et thoro,* or divorce "from bed and board," divorce did not become fully legalized in England until 1857.[9]

During the Colonial Period, this country adhered to some, but not all, of the standards of the English ecclesiastical courts. The South, for example, remained generally faithful to English tradition, and divorce was all but nonexistent. In contrast, some states north of the Mason–Dixon line did allow divorce to take place, although rarely. The New England states, for example, occasionally granted divorce, and Pennsylvania passed a law in 1682 that allowed for a "Bill of Divorcement" in cases of adultery. Other states followed suit later, Massachusetts passed a divorce law in 1786, and by 1800, every New England state, as well as New York, New Jersey and Tennessee, had legislation dealing with divorce.[10] Although the grounds for divorce varied from state to state, they were frequently restricted to adultery. However, by 1900, most states were permitting divorce for cruelty or desertion, as well as adultery.

As in English law, divorce was still very much based on morality and fault, one partner being looked on as the guilty party. Alimony was also based on guilt and innocence, and one was either rewarded or punished. For example, a woman found guilty of adultery could be denied alimony. If her husband was the adulterer, he might be required to make increased compensatory property awards to his wife.

Sex roles also played a major part in determining the grounds for divorce. Husbands were considered legally responsible for financially supporting their families, while wives were expected to take care of the domestic duties. The neglect or abandonment of these responsibilities by either spouse was viewed by some states as cruelty or desertion.

The history of traditional sex roles goes back only to the mid-1800s. Prior to that period, it was the father who was customarily awarded custody of the children since, according to common law, they were his property. Wives were also considered property and were not entitled to any control over their children, other than expecting to receive their reverence and respect.[11] This state of affairs changed with the Industrial Revolution, when men moved off the farms and into factories and offices. In 1839, Parliament modified the father's absolute right of custody by introducing the "tender years" presumption, whereby mothers were granted the right to the custody of children younger than seven.[12]

Concepts of morality and fault were to remain central in divorce proceedings well into the twentieth century, often with devastating consequences. Divorce was difficult to undergo even in the most favorable of circumstances, and bad feelings were often made worse because one spouse had to come up with grounds based on immorality (often fabricated) against the other. This happened all too often even when both parties had agreed to divorce.

NO-FAULT DIVORCE

In 1970, California passed the first law in the Western world that totally abolished fault in divorce. This new "no-fault" law required only that one party assert that "irreconcilable differences have caused the irremediable breakdown of the marriage." The justification for passing this law came out of a recognition that, in our society, divorce is sometimes inevitable and unavoidable. Other justifications were rejection of the moral framework of the traditional law, which was based on guilt or innocence; a recognition of the growing equality of women; and a desire to minimize the adversarial nature of the procedure.[13]

Divorce was no longer based on issues of moral judgment; rather, it was looked on as a private decision in which each partner was to be treated equally. It was the hope that such changes would reduce much of the acrimony surrounding divorce proceedings and, consequently, would be less destructive to the children. Within ten years, all but two states had adopted some form of no-fault law, and by 1985, all states offered no-fault divorce, even though most retained fault grounds as well.[14]

The creation of these new laws radically redefined the concept of divorce. The State, which had formerly protected marriage, was now facilitating divorce:

With this seemingly simple move, the California legisla-
ture not only vanquished the law's moral condemnation
of marital misconduct; it also dramatically altered the
legal definition of the reciprocal obligations of husbands
and wives during marriage.[15]

Theso laws were perceived as reflecting more accurately
the status quo of modern family life. The riso in divorce rates
was not viewed so much as resulting from the breakdown of
the family, but rather as providing a safety valve for the
smaller families of today, which inevitably place more demands on the individual:

The real divorce revolution, arguably, was not the passage
of the no-fault statutes. These statutes were a delayed
ratification of a system largely in place; a system that was
expensive, dirty, and distasteful.[16]

Some of these changing perceptions, although innovative, had, in fact, been anticipated by nineteenth-century theorists of family evolution. This approach saw the family as a
dynamic, rather than static, entity that develops according to
the laws of evolution and is continually subject to change.
One proponent of this theory, Lester Frank Ward (1841–1913),
saw the traditional sex roles as a product of society and
envisioned a time when women would be sharing with men
all of the responsibilities of the family, even child care. Her-
bert Spencer (1820–1903) similarly foresaw an eventual move
away from a patriarchally dominated family to one in which
there would be equality between the sexes. He also foresaw a
time when marriage would be a voluntary, contractual relationship, not based on legal restrictions or social sanctions.
An advocate of divorce, he predicted that society would eventually come to be more accepting of it, as well as to make
marital decisions with a greater degree of care.[17] Although
these sociologists were clearly ahead of their time, we have
little evidence that people are, as Spencer suggested, currently
being more careful in the selection of their mates!

Family reformers, who were opposed to this theory, saw the family as being very much at risk. They felt it was being undermined by such movements as the liberalization of women's rights and the industrialization of American society. It was divorce, however, that was looked on as the greatest threat to family survival and that dominated the literature on the family in the nineteenth century.[18]

What was not anticipated in the passage of no-fault divorce was the economic impact it was to have on some women, particularly those with young children. Although the role of women during the 1970s was very much in a state of flux, there were still many women who were primarily housewives, or who had put their careers on hold in favor of their husbands and children. In any case, many had neither the training nor the experience to earn incomes equal to those of their husbands. Before no-fault divorce, women were typically awarded more than half of the family's assets. This award was now modified to either half or an "equitable distribution." After the division of the marital property, alimony or maintenance was often time-limited, with the expectation that, after a period of readjustment, the ex-wife would get a job and become financially self-sufficient.

Although, theoretically, this arrangement made a lot of sense, in practice it did not adequately take into consideration the lower earning potential of many women, especially those who had been involved primarily in child rearing. Before the no-fault law, many men complained of having been "taken to the cleaners" by their ex-wives. Now, it was the women who were often left in financial straits. Increasingly, family homes had to be sold following divorce, because many women found themselves unable to make the mortgage payments. As a result, many more children had to deal with the loss of their homes as well as their families. Because fewer than half of all absent fathers currently pay child support, children of divorce are almost twice as likely to be living in poverty than children in intact families.[19] A study done in California in 1978 found that there was a 73 percent decline in the standard of living among women living with minor children one year after their divorce, whereas for divorced men not living with their children there was approximately a 42 percent rise.[20] In a similar study in Vermont, men's per capita income rose 120 percent following divorce, whereas women's fell 33 percent.[21] According to a report put out by the Census Bureau in 1991, income for separated families with children had declined by 37 percent four months after the separation had occurred, with only 44 percent of these families receiving child support from absent fathers one year later.[22] In the words of Betty Friedan:

> The women's movement had just begun when the so-called divorce reform law was passed . . . . We fell into a trap when we said, "No alimony!" because housewives who divorced were in terrible straits. We fell into another trap by accepting no-fault divorce without provision for mandatory economic settlements.[23]

In an effort to address these inequities, in 1984 Congress mandated that all states institute guidelines by 1987 to determine child-support awards. Included in the recommendations for these guidelines were directives that both parents share in the financial support of their children in proportion to their means.[24]

WOMEN WHO WERE LEFT

JOAN's daughter, Cathie, was just six months old when she discovered that her husband of four years was having an affair with her best friend. They subsequently divorced, and he moved to another part of the country, where he married the friend (they later also divorced). Contact over the past twelve years has been sporadic, with, at best, minimal financial support:

I felt just rageful and violated. I had supported him for six years when he was building his business. My father gave him money to go into the business. If it weren't for the fact that I had a profession and my parents were very supportive, I'm not sure what I would have done.

Joan, a slim and elegant blond with tight good looks, works as a private-duty nurse and has managed to parlay her skills into a very successful practice. This practice has enabled her to provide both for herself and for her daughter, an economically secure and comfortable lifestyle.

HELENE is vice president of a small company that produces educational material. She is a petite woman in her mid-fifties. Her short salt-and-pepper hair is stylishly cut, and she speaks with a deep, somewhat husky voice, possibly due to too much smoking. Throughout the interview she held a cigarette, sometimes lit, in her hand. The mother of two teenage children in a relatively unsatisfying marriage, she was, nonetheless, shocked when, after some seventeen years, her husband informed her he wanted to leave her. There was another woman.

It was devastating on the financial level. At that time I was in such terror and pain, not as far as love was concerned—I wasn't going to miss him that much—but I was terrified because I knew he didn't have any money. It was just very frightening. I came from a family where my father cried, "Poor, poor, poor" all the time, and I had always had a fear of being without. At the time my husband left, I was working at a low professional level, but I was very happy with my job. If I had not had a career . . . . My heart goes out to all those women who have had things like this happen who don't have a career.

I had never had a checkbook or a bank account of my own. He left me in September, and I gave him my October check. When I finally went in and opened up a bank account of my own, I walked out the door, went home—and went to bed! It was the most exhausting, traumatic thing I think I did the first couple of months. I got all my money in child support. I would not take anything in alimony. He wanted me to take it all in alimony because he figured I would be married immediately and he would cut his losses. But I wanted it in child support because I didn't have to pay taxes on the child support.

WOMEN WHO LEFT

In contrast to Joan and Helene, SANDRA was the one who initiated divorce proceedings, but not for another man:

My marriage was fraught with all kinds of tensions from the start. It took me sixteen years to decide I was going to do it. I thought you had to be married, and thank God, the women's movement came along, because I don't think I would have known that you really could be on your own. I looked around and saw other people getting divorced, and they were managing, and it was not so terrible.

Sandra's strikingly attractive appearance belies her sixty-three years. A tall, shapely woman with curly gray hair barely touching her shoulders, she has one child, a son who was twelve when her divorce was finalized sixteen years ago. Sandra has had a varied work history, mainly working in the theater and in the arts, fields known for their poor pay.

Financially, it was terribly hard because I didn't make a terrific living. My ex-husband was very much opposed to the whole thing and wasn't giving me very much. He was supposed to pay for private school, and he stopped paying. I had to take him to court. Having the financial responsibility was very hard. What was frightening, too, was having to provide Michael with certain things. I was so terrified I couldn't. Financial independence makes a tremendous difference. I think that's crucial.

114 Chapter 5

Not wanting to remarry is often not the first reaction people have following divorce. Even though Sandra had asked her husband for a divorce, her identity had been very much bound up with her role as a wife:

The hardest thing I ever did was to take off my wedding ring. It was a real trauma. I just felt that I was really a nobody, that my big claim to fame was that I was married. That was it. I felt that, whatever successes I had had in my work, my life was all tied up with being Dick's wife.

In the beginning I very much had the fantasy of getting married again, having this wonderful man who would be the guardian, the good father to my child. I wove all these fantasies around the various men whom I met—probably the first year, first couple of years. And then I just got tired of being in these relationships that really were not very rewarding and decided that it wasn't worth it. If I met somebody, fine. If I didn't, fine, too. There was a long period when I didn't go out at all, it was really fine. And then, when I went into public relations, I made tremendous friends with the people I worked with. A lot of them were single or gay, and we all had a marvelous social life together. They all liked the opera and the theater, and I was really never alone.

Sandra has been seeing someone, a widower, for the past two years:

Even now I like having my own space, having my own apartment. I like having those nights of the week when I am alone. You do get used to that. I like being with my companion, and we really enjoy each other. It's almost better, I think, when you don't see somebody every day, because it's a treat. We usually see each other three times a week, maybe four, and then we travel together.

Although Sandra is very happy with her companion and sees theirs as a long-term relationship, she has no intention of remarrying.

Some of Helene's experiences were similar:

The first couple of years were a horror for me. All I could think of was "I want to meet a man and get married." That's all I could think of. I had more blind dates than anyone. I was always falling in love instantaneously. I would either meet a man and have a ninety-day whirlwind romance and wake up one morning and hate him, or I would meet a man I would be crazy about, who would not be interested in me, and I couldn't handle it. Even though on the surface I looked as if I had everything put together, at that time I did not have a strong ego. That was the only time in my life when I could have developed a drinking problem. I just knew that I would be unhappy if there wasn't a bottle of wine in the house. I was just sipping on wine and talking to my friends on the phone. I had to either be on the phone all the time or have somebody here or go out. I just couldn't be alone.

I was the perfect example of the double person. A part of me wanted to be treated like a child and taken care of, and another part of me wanted to be very independent. I wanted my husband back; I wanted my old life back. I hated my life. I wouldn't allow myself to enjoy being alone, and I didn't allow myself to really enjoy much.

Then I met a man who was an ex-alcoholic whom I dated for about eight weeks—and then he turned on me. I went into a tailspin. I said to myself, "I have got to get out of this. This is ridiculous!" I knew how wrong it was. That's when I went into therapy. The pain that came out and the tears . . . . A year later I moved into a small apartment to cut my expenses, and I changed jobs. And that's when the big change really came. I didn't care if I went out, and I remember going for a period without a date for ten months, and I felt great.

Helene recalls a visit around that time to her son's college on parents' day. She was having dinner with him and some of his friends, together with one of his friend's parents:

The bill came, and the man took it. And I said to him, "I

insist on splitting it." He said, "I won't hear of it." And I said, "If I were a man, you wouldn't think twice, would you?" And he said, "You're right." It was an expensive restaurant, and it was a struggle for me to pay that bill, but that was a very important step for me.

Helene moved in with Steve six years ago, seven years after her husband had left her:

I am not married and feel totally strong and independent for the first time in my life. I feel very good about myself. I can't say it's idyllic, but it was something I thought I would never find in my life. I have my own separate life. I see friends away from him. He's very generous about things like that. He is separated, which is perfect for me, because I don't want ever to feel trapped into something that I can't get out of. I have grown to the point where I know any relationship is hard work on both sides. I work very hard at trying to make this work. But we've had bad times, and I remember the first ten years of my marriage. I know if something happens, there's no messy legal entanglement.

Attachment and dependency are frequently looked on as being more significant for women, partly as a result of socialization and the traditional roles women have played in society. In addition, and in contrast to men, women are commonly parented by someone of their own gender:

> Relationships, and particularly issues of dependency, are experienced differently by women and men . . . . For girls and women, issues of femininity or feminine identity do not depend on the achievement of separation from the mother or on the progress of individuation. Since masculinity is defined through separation while femininity is defined through attachment, male gender identity is threatened by intimacy while female gender identity is threatened by separation.[25]

Many women in our society still feel incomplete or deficient unless wearing the label *wife* or being involved in a relationship. Following divorce, Sandra and Helene—and no doubt, for countless others—underwent a metamorphosis into more confident, functioning women, whose sense of autonomy no longer depended on their being involved with a man. In fact, an element of distancing now appears to be built into their relationships.

JOAN had a somewhat different experience. She was raised in a traditional upper-middle-class Catholic family and married someone from a very different cultural and socioeconomic background:

I was a sixties kid, and I think my marriage was an act of rebellion. Also, I didn't know enough about what to look for. Even the day of the wedding, I knew it wasn't right, but I didn't have the courage to back out. I knew in my gut it wasn't right. I was looking for an out, I think, so when his infidelity happened, I was able to get out smelling of roses, looking like a victim. I have a wonderful child, so in that sense I have no regrets. We have a close-knit family, and they helped to make Cathie's life positive. But truly, I have raised her alone, and people accept us as a family, just the two of us.

I would never have woken up one morning and said, "I want a divorce," because I probably wasn't courageous enough. The marriage was mediocre at best. I wasn't happy, but I wasn't in despair. It wasn't unbearable, but I don't think I could have survived my whole life in that relationship. Culturally, we were just so different. There have been lonely periods, but I never regretted ending the marriage.

Even though she dated sporadically, Joan, unlike Sandra and Helene, was not especially interested in getting involved in another relationship:

The thought of juggling a man in my life, too—when and how? Make dinner for someone—what, are they nuts! I'm going to worry about someone else—more problems! Someone else I have to tend to? Where is the time or the energy? It was easier not to put in another complication. I have always felt that parenting is a serious thing. Cathie has had my unconditional attention and support. I'm always there. We've been extraordinarily close and really have had a lot of harmony. I have always been there, and she hasn't had to share me. Now that's positive and negative, but so far I think it's been positive.

During the course of our interview Joan became somewhat pensive and thoughtful:

I hope that I will meet someone and make a life for myself. When Cathie was younger, I felt I should be there because these were the nurturing years, and now she's older, I think I should be there because I don't believe teenage kids should be alone in the house all the time. What scares me is how comfortable I am by myself. When I get home, I'm exhausted. I like my privacy. My own comfort of being alone has stood in the way of my moving on and meeting people. I haven't made it a priority, clearly. I come with baggage; Cathie and I are a package. Maybe I use her as an excuse. What scares me further is how scared I am of intimacy now. It's frightening how comfortable this is, and life is so peaceful and it works. I get so frightened—what if I make another mistake? I really blew it the first time around.

I wasn't aware that I wasn't meeting my own needs all these years. I used to feel defensive. I guess I felt, "I'm doing as much as I can." I viewed getting married as taking on another responsibility.

MEN WHO WERE LEFT

Like Joan, NICK does not view a long-term relationship as a priority. A robust-looking man in his late forties, Nick wore a bow tie pulled open at the neck, which added a jovial touch to the formality of his three-piece pinstripe suit. His deep,

fruity voice has just an edge of affectation. A successful busi-
nessman, Nick married shortly after finishing graduate school.

I think I was ready to get married in the societal sense,
something that my family expected. I had no concept of
making a choice, but I definitely wanted to have a kid. She
didn't want one especially. Finally, after seven years of marriage I said, "I love you, darling, but if you don't want a kid,
I'm leaving you and will find someone who does." After
Chrissie was born, of course, she was delighted.

Nine years later, his wife informed him that she had
found someone else, saying that, besides, she felt he no longer
needed her. After a bitter court battle, joint custody was
arrived at. Chrissie, who is preparing to enter college, decided
when she was twelve that she wanted to live full time with her
father. Nonetheless, she has maintained regular contact with
her mother.
Nick has strong views about marriage today:

I think it's very difficult for a woman not to want to get
married. But there is an assumption in the term *remarriage*
that somehow marriage is a normal condition. I see myself as
living in a perfectly normal condition. I like the way it is.
Most people want to get remarried; that's probably true—that's
part of the culture. I think it's very difficult for a woman not
to want to get married. But there are different kinds of families today and the straight marriage is only one alternative. In
general, the society and even the language, with the term
remarriage, leads you to believe that most people see only one
normal condition and that everything else is an alternative
and probably a deviation from the norm.

I'm not sure why, but the idea of having only one sexual partner at a time, like being married, never seemed to
make much sense to me. I've always been a very self-sufficient person. I'm able to earn a living easily. I'm a fairly good
cook. There's nothing that I need a wife for that I can't hire. I
can hire wifely services. I think everybody, male and female,

should have a wife, someone you hire who does real wifely
things. So I don't really have any of those physical dependen-
cies that a lot of men have, who simply don't know how to
take care of themselves and seem to be intensely dependent
on having a woman. I don't really like the idea of being
married, being closed in. It puts me in a position where I am
financially responsible for the support of another adult person
with as much education as I have. I've had lots of friends,
more female than male, but a one-to-one relationship doesn't
have so much to offer. I love being alone, and I spend weekends alone by choice.

*I asked Nick if he had felt some sense of relief when his
wife left him:*
Oh, good heavens, yes!

*LAURENCE's experience was quite different from Nick's.
A tall, gently spoken and distinguished-looking man in his
early fifties, with graying hair, Laurence married his college
sweetheart after they discovered that she was pregnant. Three
children later, and after what he thought was a reasonably
compatible relationship:*

I found myself in a situation in the seventies where my
wife decided that marriage was not for her and, shortly there-
after, that parenthood was not for her. It turns out that she was
being unfaithful, and not for the first time. There had been
differences, but not the kind that I would have defined as
irreconcilable. My tendency is to be loyal. I would have
wanted to work things out. We went to a counselor, who said
that when two people are a little bit committed to working
things out, you can pull them along. When one is committed
and the other isn't, it's really tough. I don't think she was
ready to try to convince me to overlook it. That's why I think
it was deeper than just infidelity.

At the beginning, it was very anxiety-provoking, to say
the least, the uncertainty of it. On the other hand, I never

really felt totally lost. I never felt as if my life were over, that the only woman in my life was leaving me. For a woman, I think, it must be much harder.

I wanted definitely to remain single. I knew that eventually I would get married, but I didn't want to get married until my kids were grown up. I just thought it would complicate things, and my children were my top priority.

I did most of my socializing over the summer, when the children were in camp. Those were the days when sex was much freer than it is today. It was almost accepted behavior. If there was any part of being single that was difficult, it was saying no, rather than yes. I mean, there were some women who would get angry, sometimes very angry, if you said no to them, and I just didn't want to hurt their feelings.

I did enjoy it. I looked on it as a great adventure, particularly as I got married so young—because at some point I knew I'd get married, and that was going to be the end of it. I knew that my style was to be faithful.

I asked Laurence whether he thought, in retrospect, that he would have married his wife had she not been pregnant:

It's hard to say. Probably not. I don't think we were that well suited, yet there were things about us that were very well suited. But then again, the woman I married at eighteen was not the same as the woman I was married to at thirty. She was a very different person, but then, so was I.

I asked him about the influence of the women's movement:

I really think that the women's movement was just a nice way of putting a pretty face on it, because the women's movement would maybe say for a mother to be her own person and not someone's chattel her whole life, but it would not move someone in the direction of irresponsibility. I think that, even if there had not been a women's movement, this would have happened.

Six years ago Laurence met Sally and married her the following year.

The men interviewed here appear not to have found their marital breakups as traumatic as many of the women had. But then, their identities were not as inextricably bound up in their role of spouse. For some of the women, the decision not to remarry emerged only after a lengthy period during which they were faced not only with severe financial difficulties, but also with profound feelings of inadequacy and self-doubt. This was not, however, always the case.

A DIFFERENT EXPERIENCE

TERRI works as a teacher in the public school system. Dressed in blue-jean jacket, shirt, and pants and with long flowing blond hair, she looks somewhat reminiscent of the sixties, and considerably younger than her forty-eight years. Twelve years ago, the mother of two young children in a marriage gone sour, she discovered that her husband was seeing another woman:

First I was in a state of complete shock. I knew things were not good and were just deteriorating. There were all kinds of changes in his behavior; he was doing things to push me away. But I was in a state of denying and ignoring all this stuff. I was getting very high anxiety levels. I was gaining weight; I didn't look good, and I knew something was wrong. Finally, point blank, I said, "Are you involved with someone else?" He said, "I don't want to hurt you," like the classic.

I was totally paralyzed for a few days, and then I became very angry. I went immediately to a lawyer. We got divorced very quickly. It was very civil. There was no sense in my trying to make a giant fight out of this. He wanted to marry her. I realized in retrospect that I had been very unhappy, that

I was with the wrong person. He was probably very unhappy, too, but not able to articulate it. So, in a sense, he did me, personally, a favor by having this happen. I didn't want alimony, but I absolutely wanted child support.

I came to adult life at a time of tremendous foment and political change, the anti Vietnam movement and the women's movement. My mother was always a very independent woman and a very positive force for me. She wanted me to get married and have children, but she was very encouraging about my having a career and always having something that would allow me to support myself and be independent. As a child, I had always had a dream of living by myself in a penthouse. Someone was always there, a very glamorous guy, but in my fantasies in my childhood, I was living by myself.

Three weeks before we got married, I got cold feet and was very frightened of losing my independence, and I said that to him. He said, "I'm not going to take that away from you." So I said to myself, "OK, I'll get married. If it doesn't work out, I can always get divorced." This was the sixties. I guess I was very much influenced by the times. I mean, personally, I wouldn't have wanted to get divorced. But I had divorce in my family—not my mother and father—but I don't think I attached that kind of stigma to divorce.

Our society expects people to get married, and I decided that I'd had the experience of being married and that I really didn't feel I needed to be married again. I had wonderful supports. My friends and my parents were there for me. I was so independent. I was the giving one, and I discovered how to receive, how to allow other people to help me. I think that helped me tremendously to marshal my own resources. I felt so confident in myself, and I felt I was going to go on and make a new life for myself.

Terri has been involved in two long-term relationships since her divorce, one lasting for over six years. She recently broke up with a man with whom she had been seriously

*involved because he told her he could not be with someone
else's children:*

I come as a package, and that's the conflict that you get
caught in as an unmarried woman with children. I'd like to
meet a man to share my life with. I think at this stage in my
life maybe I would get married—I'm not sure why I have
changed, but after all my divorce was twelve years ago.

*CONNIE is a slender, light-skinned black woman wearing a
yellow wool suit that seems to reflect her sunny personality.
Thirty years old and the mother of six-year-old Samantha, she
works as an administrative assistant in a large Wall Street
firm. She decided not to finish college, which she was attending at night since she found herself making more money as
she worked her way up in her job. She does plan, however, to
go back at some point. Connie is the second oldest of five
children and comes from a very close-knit family:*

We have a lot of pride. Our parents instilled that in us
from when we were very little ones. They always taught us to
stand up for what we believed in: Don't be ashamed of what
you are, who you are, where you come from. The word
minority is thrown around a lot. Personally, I don't look on
myself as minority; I look at myself as a person.

*She was twenty, and her husband twenty-one, when they
got married:*

We were both young and dumb. At that point in my life,
I wanted to get married and have a baby. I thought I was
ready. After we got married, things changed. He became jealous and possessive, and it snowballed. What drove me to the
point where I wanted the divorce was that he had stopped
working, and the more he didn't work, the more possessive he
became. At some point, I decided it was not worth it to stay
in this relationship.

Connie was quite depressed for about a year following the divorce:

I wanted a stable household for Samantha, because that's what I came from, and at some point, I was angry at myself because it hadn't worked. Counseling helped me come out of the depression. I don't blame him 100 percent because we were both in the relationship, and I feel that it's never one person's fault. There was something wrong there between the two of us, so that we couldn't click after a certain point.

I went back home with my parents, and that worked out fine. When I got my own apartment, I realized that I could pay my own bills and take care of myself and my daughter fairly well. I could have a decent, stable home without a man there to tell me what to do and how to do it. And then I decided, this is what I want. I had my family around, and that's good for Samantha. So I don't need a male around putting demands on me. I can basically do it myself. I can't do it all—don't get me wrong—but I can basically fend for myself, and I am comfortable. I make my own decisions. If you are married, it's a joint thing, and you have to do these things together, and if you have a partner who is not as responsible as you are, it's hard.

At this point in my life I want to date other people. I want the opportunity to be out there and experience a lot of different guys. When I got married, I thought that was it. I would be married to this guy for the rest of my life. When it didn't work out, I said to myself, "There are lots of men out there and I should date other men." This was after I had been in a depression for about a year.

I envision myself being like this, because of the kind of person I am—very demanding, very sort of, like, set in my ways. When you live alone, there are certain things that you want done a certain way. But you never know. It might change, but now, that's how I feel. I really like the way things are. I am very content.

Chapter 6

Divorce: The Children

Children do not perceive divorce as a second
chance, and this is part of their suffering.
Judith S. Wallerstein and Sandra Blakeslee[1]

Over two million children a year are affected by divorce in this country, a figure that has more than tripled since 1960. In light of the overall decline in the birthrate during this same period, this figure is indeed impressive. As over 60 percent of divorcing couples have children, it is projected that two-thirds of all children born in wedlock since 1980 will experience some disruption due to divorce before their seventeenth birthdays.[2]

Divorcing parents are faced with two basic tasks. One is to rebuild their lives as adults, and the other is to take care of their children. Although divorce has become increasingly viewed as preferable to battling parents, the transitional period following the divorce is usually very stressful for all family members. This process may have begun years before the actual divorce and may continue for many years after. Because most of our understanding of early childhood development is based on children from intact families, it is no easy matter to predict the effects divorce will have on children:

The divorced family is an entirely new family form, one

that needs to be looked at entirely on its own . . . we need
to develop new theory.[3]

RESEARCH ON THE CHILDREN

The psychological tasks of children during this stressful
period in their lives differ by the sex and the age of the child.
Boys, for example, have been found to be more emotionally
vulnerable to marital conflict and divorce than girls, who are
generally more resistant to environmental stresses. Boys, but
not girls, whose parents separated before their fifth birthdays
have been found to have difficulties in developing a firm
sex-role identity.[4] As these findings were based on studies of
mother-headed households, they may have resulted from the
boys' lack of a readily available male role model at a critical
developmental age.

In one of the earliest longitudinal studies done on families of divorce, the California Children of Divorce Project
begun in 1971, Judith Wallerstein, Shauna Corbin, and Julia
M. Lewis did an in-depth study of sixty families over ten
years.[5] These families were largely white, middle-class, and
professional and comprised 131 children and adolescents.
Because the focus of this study was how the children of
"normally healthy families" coped with divorce, chronic problems were screened out.

The researchers found that a determining factor in the
early disturbances they saw was the age of the child at the
time of the divorce. The following is a summary of these
findings:

1. Ages 2½ to 3¼ showed regressive behavior.
2. Ages 3¾ to 4¾ manifested aggressive behavior, bewil-
   derment, irritability, and self-blame.
3. Ages 5 to 6 displayed high levels of anxiety and aggressive behavior.

4. Ages 7 to 8 manifested conflicting feelings of anger and loyalty to both parents, as well as sadness, grieving, fear, and fantasies of responsibility and reconciliation.
5. Ages 9 to 10 showed feelings of loss, rejection, helplessness, loneliness, shame, anger, and conflicts about loyalty.
6. Adolescents (age 11 and over) were preoccupied with feelings related to individuation from their parents and worries about their own future. They exhibited behavior patterns of withdrawal and expressed feelings of sadness, shame, and embarrassment.[6]

Preschool children were most affected early in the breakup, and little boys were more distressed than little girls. These sexual disparities lessened over time, however, and this age group seemed less burdened in later years than the other age groups. They did not usually have memories of fighting or conflict, but they did have fantasies of what it might have been like to grow up in an intact family. In contrast, older children (late latency and adolescence at the time of the divorce) saw their parents' divorce as having had a major effect on their lives. Many of them retained vivid memories of unhappy family experiences and had restrained feelings of sadness. Overall, one-third of the total sample was clearly doing well five years later, whereas well over a third of the children were significantly worse off.

Although Wallerstein *et al.* expected the negative effects of divorce to have dissipated ten years after the divorce, this was not the case. Many of the children were doing poorly at the ten-year mark. A significant number were troubled or drifting, and a third of the women were wary of entering into lasting relationships with men. Based on their findings, the researchers concluded that the negative effects of divorce on children were more long-standing and deleterious than had previously been thought.

These findings have generated considerable controversy.

Some critics have felt that the study presented a far more negative picture of the effects of divorce than other research suggests, that the sample was not sufficiently representative of the children of divorce as a whole, that not enough attention was paid to the negative effects of the reduced finances of the family, and that the children may have been having problems not necessarily related to the divorce. For example, the adolescent children may have been having difficulties related more to the turmoil of adolescence than to the marital status of their parents. Moreover, the quality of the relationships the child retained with both parents was far more critical in their positive adjustment than the details of custody arrangements.[7]

Wallerstein *et al.* found a strong correlation between the overall quality of life of the family and how well the children did psychologically. This finding has been substantiated by other studies. One longitudinal study[8] that followed a group of children who were of nursery school age when their parents divorced found the first year following the divorce to be the most difficult. However, if the children were living in a relatively stable and conflict-free home, their behavior generally improved over the course of the second year. In fact, children living in low-conflict divorced families compared favorably with children coming from high-conflict intact families.

Other research suggests that interpersonal conflicts, rather than the separation or divorce per se, are the major causes of behavioral problems in children. In one study of white divorced middle-class families,[9] when the parents were able to cooperate on issues related to the children, earlier behavioral problems among latency-age children were significantly diminished.

As mentioned earlier, an important predictor of how successfully children will cope with the impact of divorce is the parent–child relationship. A good relationship has been cited as the most powerful influence on behavioral and school adjustment and can greatly mitigate the negative effects of the divorce.[10] A close relationship with even one parent is extremely important. And when there is continued antagonism between the parents, as is often the case, if the parents are able to keep these problems separate from their concerns for their children, the children are less likely to be adversely affected.

It appears, then, that some children benefit from divorce when they have been exposed to high levels of conflict in the family. However, tensions and hostilities often escalate following divorce, and the children are caught in the crossfire, leaving them even more exposed to conflict and divided loyalties than ever. Only if the parents are able to cooperate in what is in the best interests of the children is it possible to prevent the long-term effects and suffering that result from the dissolution of the family.

MOTHERS AND THEIR CHILDREN

JOAN's husband left her when her Cathie, now fourteen, was an infant:

My sense is that she has had a very happy childhood. I'm convinced beyond any shadow of a doubt that she has had it much easier than children who have to deal with divorce at fourteen, or ten. She was spared that agony. A lot of her friends' parents are getting divorced now, and it's really hard for them. She recently said to me, "I never had the turbulence. I never saw the anger. I've never experienced any of that." She hasn't experienced parents who fight, or fighting with a brother or sister. She hasn't had a parent who had to say, "You have to wait your turn." I have been there for her. The basic disagreements that I had with my ex-husband would have created a lot of ambivalence for her. We really have had a lot of harmony.

The fact is that she hasn't had a father here. Her father's like a visiting uncle. Maybe he sees her three times a year. I suspect a boy would have missed the presence of a father more. I sometimes worry about how she'll see men because she sees men coming and going, but I haven't had that many men in my life, for sure. My father and my brother have been an important part in our lives. She goes to private school. I picked a coed one because it was important for her to have boys around her.

I really felt she didn't ask to be the product of a divorce. I don't want her to pay too high a price. As a result, I have really gone out of my way to make her life normal. The thing I regret most about being divorced, for Cathie's sake, is the fact we don't eat dinner as a family. I eat dinner with her, but I always think a family has to have a mom and dad and six kids around the table.

I think Cathie is better off. But be forewarned, the task is awesome. There are lonely moments; there are those times when I need someone to talk to. I sometimes just need another set of hands. It's sometimes so hard to make a decision alone. But it clearly can work, and we are one example.

CONNIE's daughter was three when she broke up with her husband:

At the time that I was filing for divorce, I felt I didn't really want him to have anything to do with me or Samantha, either. That came from a lot of animosity and anger that was inside me, which I realize now was wrong. Because he is, after all, her father, no matter what happens.

He doesn't see her regularly. She doesn't understand why she doesn't have him around. The other kids in school want to know about her father, and she's always asking about him. I think it's much harder for my daughter to deal with this than it is for me. A little boy in her class was crying because he didn't know where his father was. I said to her, "Did that bother you?" and she said, "Yes, because I don't know where my daddy is, either."

My father's there, and my brothers are there, which has

been helpful, because I worry about having a father figure around. I want her to be a well-rounded person. Even though I am there for her, she still needs that balance, that male figure in her life. It can't all be mummy.

Being a single parent, you bear the whole burden all alone. Basically, I am on my own, but my family is still there, and I am very fortunate that I have them. It's good for me as an individual, but I can't say it's so good for my daughter. But for the most part, she's OK.

In spite of the modifications in custody awards, which no longer automatically give preference to the mother, women continue overwhelmingly to be the custodial parent. Like Cathie and Samantha, growing numbers of children are having little contact with their noncustodial fathers following divorce, although this is not as true when the noncustodial parent is the mother. Recent studies indicate that a substantial and growing fraction of noncustodial fathers are not only spending minimal time with their children but offering them little in the way of material and emotional support.[11] This lack of contact occurs particularly when the father remarries and starts a new family, but not always.

TERRI's children were eight and two when she was divorced. Although her ex-husband remarried almost immediately, starting a new family with his second wife, he has maintained regular and ongoing contact with his children:

We worked out a joint-custody agreement. He has had them with him for all these years every Thursday night and every other weekend.

I asked how this arrangement suited the kids:

Well, I think that we want to think most children are very resilient and adapt very easily. But I have seen over the years the ramifications of our getting divorced. When Jay was eight, he started to feel that he never remembered when his parents were married. He felt this terrible conflict about who was his real father, because I was involved with a guy I met right after my husband and I split up. Jay said, "I can't remember when you and daddy were married, and I sometimes think that Hank is my real father."

We sometimes lived together, sometimes not. We were "apart-ners." He kept his apartment, and I kept mine. The kids wanted us all to live together. First, the kids wanted mummy and daddy to get back together. Then, they wanted us all to live together in one big house. Mary hated Hank. She was nine when Hank and I got involved. She managed to decide that she couldn't stand him and did everything she could to undermine him. When she was twelve, she was not doing well at school. She started to talk about suicide. She was not truly suicidal, but she was using it as a way to get help. We got her into treatment, and I had to put her into a private school. She hasn't done well all the way along.

I asked how much of this Terri thought was related to the divorce:

Quite a bit. I think that had a very dramatic effect. When all this happened, people were getting divorced right and left. We expect children to be very resilient. We want them to adjust, but this can't be. Mary had so many fears about loss and abandonment. Her whole development and maturity level were almost arrested. She was afraid to grow up.

Divorce was good for me, but not so good for the kids. I certainly hope that both of them will eventually be with someone whom they find companionship and support from.

On the other hand, in spite of her own anxiety, SANDRA felt that Michael benefited from her deciding to leave her husband.

I think it was honestly a relief for him. I don't know what he would have been like had we stayed together. I know that I would have been a wreck. Michael was twelve and I think it was really damaging for him that we stayed together so long, because there was so much constant friction. We were really at cross purposes all the time. Maybe, had I been stronger and different, it would have been easier if I'd split earlier, because by the time a child is twelve, the behavior patterns are set. I think he's had a very hard time; it's been very tough. Certainly, being in this relationship—we never really agreed on how we should raise this child—certainly couldn't help at all. I don't know whether it was any worse during the period when we were divorcing. After the divorce, Michael didn't speak to his father for a very long time. So that made it very hard.

Sandra sadly notes that Michael has carried his problems into his adult life:

We don't even know how important genes are. It used to be all the impact of the mother. I was a very anxious parent who didn't know a whole lot about being a mother. I think I was overprotective, so that didn't help. I know there's this theory that divorce damages children beyond repair and all that sort of thing, but I think that children who are going to be damaged will be damaged.

For me, at least, any decisions I made were my decisions, so in that sense it was easier. I didn't have to consult my ex and be at war with him about what we were going to do with our child. We were always at loggerheads, even after we split up.

I think the sadness is to marry somebody because you want to have children. I very much wanted a child, and my thought was that I had to be married to have one. I had such romantic ideas of being a parent that it never entered my mind that I was going to have the troubles I had.

It would have been better for everybody if we had got along, if we had all been different people, or if we had been at different stages in our lives.

HELENE *felt so overwrought when her husband left her that it was hard for her to focus on the children:*

When this happened, I was not the greatest mother. But my children, aged ten and twelve, were very independent. They were like weeds; they were busy with their own lives. I didn't worry about them because I knew my husband would provide for them. In all fairness, George was a wonderful father.

The first few months, they both tried to sleep in bed with me, which I never allowed, never once. The youngest child gave me a very hard time the first year. I remember he said to me, "I hate you. I'm glad Daddy left you. You are fat and ugly, and I hate you!" You don't know how you are going to react, but I had no problem with it. I felt this was very normal. He was very angry. It didn't hurt me, but I felt sad. He was always a very difficult child, but that was not related to the divorce. He always stepped to the tune of a different drummer.

I didn't enjoy my children when they were little. I never had a strong desire to be a mother, ever. Going to work, I think, saved me a great deal, and once I put myself together, I began to appreciate my children.

As we talked, Helene began to reflect more about the children:

They used to worry about me a great deal. I cried a lot, but I was unhappy and miserable. It must have been very rough for them. They worried about me; they were frightened about me. They must have gone through a lot of pain as I think back about it, the way I was.

A FATHER'S EXPERIENCE

LAURENCE *had already moved out of the family home when his wife decided to give him custody of their three latency-aged children. She moved out and he moved back in:*

I knew that she was building up to be able to say, "I don't want the kids." In a sense, I feel as if I might have manipulated it by making it very easy for her. Then again, I could have manipulated all night and all day and it wouldn't have done me any good if she wanted the kids.

I asked how the children had handled the separation:

I think the kids felt great anxiety about it because, after all, they were not very experienced in life. There was the uncertainty of something they had not been aware of before. But absolutely, it was a relief to them when I moved back. I was always very much involved. I was the father who got up Saturday mornings and took the kids out. She had a hard time getting up in the morning. So we just left her and we went to the park. When their mother left, she left. She's had periodic contact, but only when it's convenient. They look on her now as being a kind of superficially pleasant aunt.

At the beginning it was very anxiety-provoking. My mother tried to help out, but there was a heavy price to pay, so I moved off of that. I came from a broken home as well. I had a very good father, but my mother is kind of a neurotic. The children have an aunt who is a very substantial person. She was the only one who was ever totally supportive.

I organized my life around the children. I brought my business to within four blocks of my home, which I was lucky to be able to do. I would get up in the morning with the kids and organize their day. I would very often take off lunchtime to do the marketing. The kids would come to my office and meet me every day.

Sometimes I had help and sometimes I didn't. You do what you have to do. They pitched in like other kids, nothing special. I always felt that I didn't want them to be disadvantaged by having only one parent. I had to compensate a lot. I didn't want my kids to suffer for their mother.

Andrea, the eldest—she was almost twelve when her mother left—was very needy. She cut school, which was definitely related to the divorce. It began before the separation, but after, it got worse. I think it delayed her adolescence. She was the one who was the most vulnerable. If she saw me with a nice woman, she would warm up to her. Certain women saw that as a vulnerability on my part and I think took advantage of it, which was kind of unfair. So I stayed very guarded, and after a time, I kept women away. Theo, the middle one, went through a period in fifth grade when he wasn't doing well, either.

Laurence feels that, with help, these difficulties were eventually overcome with no discernible long-lasting effects:

If they had their druthers, I think they would prefer to have had a normal home. I think, very importantly, the kids always were very sure of me. The one thing that I think is important is that there was always terrific communication between me and my kids, because there was always a feeling among all of us that we were all in this together, even at the times when things were most stressful. They always knew that I was never going to do anything that was ever going to break up the family. The biggest problem, whether there are two parents at home, or fourteen parents, or one, is, if your kids sense that they're on one side of the world and you're on the other, you're in trouble.

What made it easier was that I had good kids. The only time they gave me a hard time is that I could never find out who messed up the kitchen, because each one would say it was one of the others!

JOINT CUSTODY

Following on the heels of the 1970 no-fault divorce laws came changes in the rules determining custody. A major shift was away from giving automatic preference to the mother, especially in cases of children of "tender years," namely chil-

dren below the age of seven, to a rule that was sex-neutral and
based on the child's "best interest." In 1980, California became the first state to institute joint custody, and by 1984,
thirty states had adopted some form of joint-custody legislation. Relatively few fathers, in fact, have opted for sole custody, and mothers overwhelmingly continue to have physical
custody of their children.[17] However, growing numbers of
parents are now sharing legal custody.

In cases of joint, or shared, legal custody, the children
usually have a primary abode with one parent, and the parents share in the basic decision making. Joint physical custody implies that the children spend equal time between two
households, and that the parents participate equally in their
day-to-day care. Two of the logistical requirements are a relatively close proximity between the two households and a very
high degree of cooperation between the parents. In addition,
there is the expense of having two sets of clothing, toys, and
so on. It is not, therefore, surprising that shared physical
custody is the exception, rather than the rule.

We are going to look at two situations of joint custody:
One appeared to have been quite successful, and the other
had met with only limited success.

NICK had always been a very involved parent:

I would think that the single male parents you find are
people who have been involved with raising their children
from the time of conception on. They are nurturers, but that
doesn't necessarily exclude their ex-spouses. I was not a father who came home and spent thirteen minutes with my kid
I knew the name of the kindergarten teacher. I was the helping
"mummy" at the day care center.

So I was very shocked when my ex-wife said, "I want you
to leave, and I want sole custody of Chrissie." The notion that
I could be separated from my child, physically or psychologically, with any less devastation than my wife would feel was
absurd. I wasn't the "other parent." The concept of equal

parents was something that I think was understood in our marriage. It was very clear.

My lawyer told me that if I walked out of the door, I didn't have a kid, and he was right. We went for joint custody, and she went along with it because she didn't have a choice. Chrissie was then nine. We wound up living in the same house with joint custody for two years in separate bedrooms. We both had schedules drawn up. I had my morning, and she had her morning. I couldn't move out because, had I done so, I would have been treated as a normal father, and I would have wound up with very generous visitation, which would have driven me absolutely bananas, visiting my own child.

Chrissie hated it. She went into withdrawal. She just shut it off. She would crawl right inside herself, went around with a glazed look in her eyes. I was stressed out.

After the end of the two years, my ex-wife couldn't stand it anymore. She brought an action to accelerate the custody portion of the trial. She was going for sole custody. We had a court-appointed psychiatrist, all those little games. I hired a psychiatrist to teach me how I should dress and so on. She was moving out of state to get married, and the judge found an old statute saying that preference goes to the parent who lives in the same state. So she lost, and the judge told us to settle for joint custody, which I wanted from the beginning.

Chrissie lived with both of us, one week on, one week off, which worked out rather well. Everyone made it pretty clear that she had two homes. When she was with me, I dropped her off at school. When she was with her mother, her mother had to hire a driver to take her to school and back. After about a year, Chrissie wanted to make it two weeks.

When she was twelve she decided she wanted to live with me full time. She was tired of the commuting, and it really became tiresome, two weeks here, two weeks there. It was a real hassle. Friends became a big issue. I wanted her to go to a local school where she could have neighborhood friends. I was aware of the problems mothers and daughters have at that age, and if that's what it was, then I wasn't going to agree to it. But it was more than that. She didn't like her stepfather, for one thing. Her mother threatened to go back to court again, but I made it clear it was my intention to help work out what Chrissie wanted. It got nasty, but it worked out. Chrissie still sees her mother two days a week.

What I noticed immediately was that Chrissie and I stopped having conflicts right away. I never had really noticed before that the conflicts had had to do with me and my ex-wife, rather than with Chrissie and me. I do think that the joint custody impacted on her feeling of having roots. One of the things she is looking forward to in college is that she will have only one place that she has to be.

Chrissie is an extremely well-adjusted kid. She's got everything going for her, so, as to detrimental effects, I don't know where they are. But boyfriends are a real problem. She's had one boyfriend, but it didn't work out.

I asked how joint custody was for him:

I think it's great, if you can afford it. It's like a limo service back and forth with a driver. When I had one week on and one week off, I had the best of all possible worlds. I was a bachelor one week and a daddy the next. My women friends knew that was the way it was, and it worked out unbelievably.

What about now?

I don't have to deal with someone else. I don't have to discuss with someone else how I should raise my child. I've got a one-to-one relationship with my child, which makes things much, much easier. And if you're disposed to be child-centered in the first place, it works out very well. I never saw Chrissie as a child; she was always the other person there. A single parent of a sole child is a particular kind of relationship. It's one-to-one. The kid has all your attention, and you have all the kid's attention. You develop a relationship that is probably different from a single parent of two children or two parents with one child. You can't not develop it; it works out that way.

TAMAR, a social worker, had been married for thirteen years to a college professor when her marriage just did not seem to be working anymore:

Our communication had completely shut down. We were spending more and more time apart from one another. Lizzie, our youngest, was still very small. Ever since she has been born, things hadn't been that good. The tensions were probably simmering. It's hard for me to know exactly when I started realizing how unhappy I was. I attributed a lot of my unhappiness to the marriage. I talked about it with Charles, and I sort of expected him not to go for the idea of divorce as quickly as he did. But as soon as I told him, it was clear that he was unhappy, too. We tried to talk to one another a lot. It cleared the air a little, but it wasn't a marriage anymore.

Tamar's manner, like her dress, is low-key and relaxed. Her bushy hairstyle and casual sweater and pants indicate someone not especially concerned with appearances:

We were very amicable, right from the beginning. We were discussing this joint-custody thing. The children were four and seven. We didn't do that badly as parents. It's just as husband and wife that we did badly. I thought Charles was a terrific father, and I think he thought I was a terrific mother. We were very rational and thoughtful when it came to approaches to child rearing; we had the same values. Our conflicts didn't interfere with our ability to deal with the kids. We could separate them; I don't really know why.

By the time we talked to the children, we had already worked out when they would see us. One of the reasons I wasn't ready to divorce Charles was that, because my father had died when I was twelve years old, I couldn't bear depriving my children of a father. I really thought that for Steven, especially, it was just very important to have a father. I also felt that children don't really care, that the emphasis on the actual physical space is not that important to them. I thought it was completely misunderstood by people who assumed that the room and the toys and the space are what make a stable home.

What makes a stable home is parents, and as long as they could keep their parents, even if they lost part of their physical home, that was preferable. The sadness that I thought they would feel if they saw their father only on weekends was just too much. The relationship with their parents should change as little as possible. As long as the children were small, it just seemed ridiculous that they would care what their room looked like. I thought if they could see Mummy and Daddy every day, then they wouldn't feel the loss so much, so that's the way we worked it out.

Charles found an apartment, luckily, in the neighborhood, and we all went over together to not make it seem as if anybody was being kicked out. I remember walking with a shopping cart with sheets and towels and helping to make the beds there. It was a sacrifice on my part. I came home and cried.

They saw us every day. If they saw me in the morning, they saw him in the evening. We could have done one week here, one week there, but that seemed more disruptive, so we alternated every other day. There was a regularity to it; every Monday was the same as every other Monday. Monday evening they would see Daddy, Tuesday morning Daddy would send them off to school, and then they would come back to me after they were picked up from the after-school group. Weekends we split. That's when we would see one another.

Believe me, people thought I was crazy. People thought it was absolutely wrong. But in a very deep way, the kids really came first. We were responsible for raising these human beings, and we had to be adults about it. And if we didn't, we just didn't deserve to be parents.

We had talked about the need to be as close as possible to be able to pull it off. We didn't even have a formal separation agreement. We just sat down and typed out one sheet that the children would spend half the time with each parent. We never had a lawyer. The actual filing of divorce papers was very inexpensive—I think it was something like seventy dollars. It's just a lot of papers. If people realized, it's not that difficult.

We had to duplicate everything. They had enough toys at both places. Sometimes, that was the only thing that was an inconvenience, like occasionally all the winter jackets would end up in one place. Occasionally, it gets completely unbalanced.

The kids didn't really seem to suffer. The way Charles and I had been living earlier, we were alternating anyway. We never really did things much as a family, but they got a lot of attention. Ironically, they agree with me now, because we have talked about it, that they may have got better parenting than from people who were together. We weren't diverted. On the nights I had them, I really was here for them. I was really actually better able to be with them because I had those other nights off. It was wonderful, and I needed that break.

I always arranged my time on the night I didn't have the kids. I had a good deal. I didn't realize what the perk would be for me, but it really was a terrific perk. If I had had the children here full time I just don't know what I would have done, because I had a pretty stressful job. I worked every day, and I had a lot of responsibility. Charles said it was so much more work for him, and I said it was so much easier for me. But it wasn't only the parenting. He had done a lot of that, but he really hadn't had to clean the house, and wash the dishes, and make the meals, and do the shopping, and think about the lunches the next day.

I think the kids are doing fine. There certainly weren't any noticeable problems that I remember. There was a period when they hoped we would get back together again. They did keep fantasizing that for a couple of years. It didn't make sense to them. Maybe it confused them a little bit that we were so friendly. There were some disagreements that Charles and I had, but they were exactly the same kinds of disagreements we would have had if we were married, I think.

I imagined that, when the kids got to be a certain age, like teenagers, they wouldn't go for this joint-custody arrangement anymore. In the back of my mind, I thought that, when they got to be teenagers, the space would become more important again. I wasn't going to bring it up, and they haven't brought it up. I expected to have a more dramatic change in many ways when they became teenagers, but their anchors are still with us. They get along with kids at school, but they don't have friends. I have no idea why. Maybe it's because they don't have the space. Maybe they are very busy, and maybe it has nothing to do with the divorce. Maybe it's just the kind of people they are.

SUMMARY

We have seen that there are many reasons why people decide not to remarry. No doubt a larger sample would have produced even more examples. The parents interviewed here are currently doing quite well in their lives. Many felt that going through a divorce, although a painful experience, resulted in their becoming more confident and self-assured. Many described their children as doing well; others did not.

What these interviews suggest is that, generally, the parents seem to be doing better than the children, who are inevitably at greater risk, stand to lose more as the result of the divorce, and some feel as if their childhood has been lost forever.[13]

Chapter 7

Homosexuality and Parenthood

> *The things which motivate homosexuals to*
> *become parents are precisely the same things*
> *which motivate heterosexuals to become parents.*
> Roberta Achtenberg[1]

Homosexuality is not generally thought of in conjunction with parenthood. First of all, it is biologically impossible for two same-sexed partners to conceive a child together. Second, the stereotype of the homosexual lifestyle—the world of the bars, being pleasure-loving, promiscuous, and uncommitted—is not easily seen as synonymous with the nurturing role associated with parenting.

Nonetheless, it is estimated that, in the United States, there are three to five million gay and lesbian parents, raising eight to ten million children. Many of these parents have previously been married and only later came to openly recognize their homosexuality, both to themselves and to others.

I met STANLEY in his comfortable eastside apartment in upper Manhattan, where he lives with his daughter, Linda, who is eighteen. His son, Paul, twenty-one, is currently away at school. *Stanley is forty-eight, Jewish, and a lawyer by profession. When he was in his early twenties, he went to see a psychiatrist because he was having sporadic homosexual fantasies that made him feel very anxious. The psychiatrist told him that such fantasies were completely normal and convinced him that he was heterosexual. Reassured, Stanley got married shortly after, had two children, and proceeded to live a reasonably satisfying married life, which included enjoying sexual relations with his wife. After nine years, his wife, an ardent feminist (this was the early 1970s), wanted to leave the marriage, which had been going sour anyway. They managed to agree on joint custody for the children. Joint custody did not work out well because the children seemed to be constantly on the move, so that when his wife decided to leave the state, the children decided to live with their father. This was good for Stanley, who had always been very involved with his children and wanted to continue to play an active role in their lives.*

After the breakup, he dated several women, one in particular whom he liked very much. However, he started noticing that he was again having fantasies about wanting to have sex with men. He again sought out a therapist but this time would not be persuaded that he was not gay. He remembers feeling that the therapist was having distinct difficulties with this idea, and his contact with the therapist was brief:

I very quickly came to the realization that I was gay. I was not experienced in knowing gay people or gay culture. I was very frightened of the switch because it was all very forbidding and looked down upon.

CHARLENE, a divorced mother of eighteen-year-old Lance, is a handsome-looking, light-brown-skinned woman of forty-two with finely sculpted classic features. She is one of four children born to a West Indian family that settled in New Jersey, where she was born. Charlene attended college, specializing in education, in which she has a master's degree.

When Charlene was in her mid-twenties she met and fell in love with Tony, whom she later married and with whom she bore her son. Previously, while still in graduate school, she had met another female student to whom she had become very close. When this relationship developed into a sexual one, Charlene still did not consider herself a homosexual. Rather, she viewed this relationship as an aberration, a crush:

I totally denied the homosexual part of myself. Everything I read and saw in the media about homosexuality was negative, and that was not me. It was deviant, it was bad, it was against society.

Nonetheless, she continued seeing her friend, Leah, but did not share with her husband her double life. Three years after her son was born, and because of her husband's increasing involvement with alcohol, she decided to get a divorce. It was only then that she began to confront her lesbianism and to start on a journey that she has not yet completed:

It's something you discover about yourself in early childhood, but you're not supposed to speak about or even acknowledge it. I used to wonder why I was feeling this way, and I didn't understand where it was coming from. Although I was shocked inside I felt I had come home.

A BRIEF HISTORY

The word *homosexual* has a long history of pejorative use. Consequently, the gay community disdains its use as a term by which to define people. Other reasoning against its use is that it offers too narrow a perspective. One does not usually refer to someone as heterosexual as a way of describing who they are; why, then, should one do that with someone who is gay? The terms *gay* and *lesbian* are the common usage today. Although *gay* can be used more generally to refer to both men and women, *lesbian* refers only to women. The word *gay* comes from the Provençal word *gai* which was used in the thirteenth and fourteenth centuries to refer to courtly love, which was often explicitly homosexual. The word *gay* connotes sexual looseness in many European countries and was first used in the United States outside the realm of pornographic literature by Cary Grant in the 1939 movie *Bringing Up Baby*.[2] In one scene, he wore a negligee and exclaimed, "I just went gay all of a sudden." The word *lesbian* comes from the Greek island of Lesbos, home of the great classical poet Sappho, who wrote romantic poetry, some of it on female homosexuality.

As attitudes toward homosexuality have changed in recent years and become somewhat more tolerant—sadly, in part because of the AIDS epidemic, and as gays themselves have become more self-accepting—an increasing number have been deciding to have families. For the first time in this country, we are seeing an openly gay middle class, a number of whom are choosing to become parents. Most commonly, they achieve parenthood either through adoption or by artificial insemination, sometimes referred to as *alternative insemination,* as gays do not consider it "artificial." More rarely, a gay man and a lesbian woman may decide to conceive a baby together, and in yet other instances, several people may decide to raise a child together, either through adoption or through one of them inseminating.

SARA is a slightly overweight, pretty, and soft-spoken woman. The day we met was extremely hot, and Sara came wearing shorts. Although they were not especially flattering, nonetheless she had a bright and cheerful appearance. She was thirty-nine when she was inseminated almost five years ago and gave birth to Justin. As she saw the biological clock ticking, she decided, "Now or never." She was very happy, as she had always wanted a son. Although she was not in a love relationship at the time, she would have preferred to be.

Sara was born in Oklahoma and went to an Ivy League school, where she studied communications. She comes from a fairly traditional family; her mother was a housewife, and her father was in the restaurant business. She has one older brother and a large extended family, to whom she is very close:

I was quite a tomboy when I was about eight or ten and wished I had been a boy, but when I was in sixth grade and boys started telling me how pretty I was, I thought, "This is great!"

She became sexually active in her early twenties and was once almost engaged to be married. However, it was not until she was in her mid-twenties that she first acted on her homosexual feelings, and only after realizing that she had been attracted to women for some time:

I said to myself, "Oh, my god, that's what's been going on!" Although I was all shaken up, inside it just felt right.

She describes her experience with the sperm bank, which she did not tell that she was gay. In any case, they did not ask:

The director told me they usually worked only with couples, but if a woman was financially and emotionally secure, they would work with her. That's ridiculous! After meeting with me for only ten minutes, the man gave me a list of the characteristics of three men: grade-point average and major and minor in college, hobbies, coloring, and religion. He wouldn't let me write down any of it. Wanted me to think of it as DNA, which I took to mean "daddy not available."

JOHN came to my office to be interviewed, having asked if I would mind if he brought eighteen-month-old Jeffrey with him. He arrived carrying Jeffrey on his shoulders, one hand alert to steady him and the other carrying a large tote bag filled with the inevitable baby paraphernalia. He is a slim

young man who wore figure-hugging bicycling shorts and a
sports shirt, and his light brown hair and rimless spectacles
framed his scrubbed good looks.

When Jeffrey, a delightful-looking brown-skinned child,
was set down on the floor, he was immediately attracted to
the toy shelf in my office. After tentatively looking me over, he
proceeded to pull the toys off the shelf and began to play. The
ease with which John related to him quickly became apparent.
At one point, Jeffrey tripped on a toy and was about to cry.
John quietly told him to pick himself up, while reassuring him
that he was OK, and the moment passed.

John is the youngest of five children and grew up in an
actively Methodist family in the Boston area. His mother was
a housewife and his father a successful businessman. John
attended college and, like his father, went into business:

I knew I was gay when I was sixteen and have been
comfortable ever since. I was a bit effeminate, and there was
a lot of taunting in school. I had to fight my way through high
school and college. I always wanted a child and am very
proud to be a parent.

Jeffrey, who is of Mexican extraction, was adopted shortly
after birth from an adoption agency in the Midwest whose
policy is to be open to potential single parents. The people at
the agency do not know that John is gay, but he suspects that
they might.

John is thirty-two and owns his own restaurant. He took
six weeks off to care for Jeffrey when he first got him and now
is able to work part time so as to care for his son. When he is
at work, Jeffrey is cared for by a local baby-sitter, but John
likes to take Jeffrey around with him as much as possible.
John says, "I probably spend more time with Jeffrey than
many heterosexual couples who both work."

He may well be right. We will return to Stanley, Charlene,
Sara, and John in the following chapter.

Not everyone in the gay community is happy with the recent growth of gay families. Having struggled to reach some level of recognition and equity in a generally homophobic society, some gays feel that those who are opting to become parents—or "breeders," as they call them—are trying to "out-straight" the straight community. By taking on conventional values, they are losing sight of their own authentic identity.

This kind of viewpoint is commonly seen among oppressed groups that are struggling for self-identity and recognition and seem to be especially directed at the newer group of gay parents, people like Sara and John. People in this situation must consequently contend with criticism from segments not only of the straight but also of the gay community. While some in the gay community see them as selling out, skepticism in parts of the straight community questions the viability of a two-mummy, two-daddy or a no-mummy, no-daddy family.

Some within the lesbian community, moreover, have negative feelings toward men. As Charlene put it:

> There are some women who are lesbian who hate men and who will have nothing to do with men. And probably, they hate women who will have a child through a man. They don't mind you going through artificial insemination, but if you have a child the natural way, the animosity is there.

Another viewpoint looks on the growing numbers of gays having children as a normalization process. Lesbians and gays are simply people who happen to be homosexual, and who have the same dreams, wishes, and aspirations as everyone else. One of these is to procreate and have children.

However one views these families, they cannot be, nor should they be, ignored. The *Kinsey Reports*[3,4] in the late forties and early fifties informed us of a much higher prevalence of homosexual experiences in our society than had previously been known, and current estimates suggest that approximately 10 percent of the population is gay.

There are about twenty-five million gays and lesbians in this country, and a third of the lesbian women are thought to be mothers. As the women's and gay liberation movements have enabled both women and gays to develop a greater sense of confidence and pride in themselves, many more gays have "come out." As this trend continues, it is inevitable that more than mere acknowledgment from society will be sought by gay parents.

DEVIATION OR NORM?

Homosexuality is as old as history itself. There are no known cultures in which homosexuality has not existed. Homosexual behavior has also been found in all animal species that have been studied in any depth.[5]

Attitudes toward homosexuality have varied over time. Although ancient Greece accepted the notion that people were bisexual, and the pre-Christian world was generally tolerant of homosexuality, most Western societies following the cue of Judaism and Christianity, have subsequently looked on it as a deviation or perversion. Homosexuality has been viewed as an oddity or a curiosity, and as defeating procreation, which Western religions have regarded as the primary purpose of sexuality.[6] The bulk of the literature and research on homosexuality has, since the turn of the century and until quite recently, supported the notion that homosexuality is a sickness, the product of a disturbed upbringing or a genetic malfunction. Homosexuals have generally been thought to have come from a dysfunctional family, to be fixated at an early level of psychological development, to be confused about their gender identity, and generally not to be whole people. Hence, those who have discovered themselves to be gay did so against the backdrop of a pathological view of homosexuality.

In contrast to the extensive literature on male homosexuality, not more than a dozen or so scattered references to lesbianism can be found during the medieval and early modern European period. In the Europe of the mid-seventeenth century, people had extreme difficulties dealing with the idea of lesbianism. Society's view of sexuality even then tended to be phallocentric, so that although women might be attracted to men, and men to men, a woman was felt to have little to offer that could long sustain the sexual interest of another woman.[7] Sexual intimacies between women, however, such as at the courts of France, were at times even tolerated, as long as they were viewed as a form of foreplay preceding heterosexual activity.

In efforts to seek causality, homosexuality has been viewed alternately as a problem of hormonal abnormality, chromosomal irregularity, gender-role-identity confusion, oedipal fixation, and family dysfunction, to name but a few views. Current theories on etiology tend to be multifaceted, inasmuch as no single constellation or factor appears to explain adequately why one person is heterosexual and another homosexual. Although today many view the very search for causes as an admission that homosexuality is a condition that needs a cure, most recent viewpoints suggest the presence of a genetic or constitutional predisposition that, combined in some cases with environmental factors, leads to same-sex attraction.[8]

In his exhaustive study on the psychoanalytic literature on homosexuality, Kenneth Lewes[9] traced attitudes from Freud to the present. He found three general views in the literature: one that sees homosexuality as an illness that limits the capacity to function well in society; a second that views it as a characteristic of other pathological states; and a third that sees it as not necessarily connected to pathology at all.

Freud appeared somewhat undecided in his position on homosexuality. Although he saw a homosexual object choice as a turning away from what he considered normal development (which culminated in a heterosexual object choice), he was not clear to what extent homosexuality was to be considered pathological. In a letter to his biographer, Ernest Jones,[10] he disagreed with Jones that a homosexual should be precluded from becoming a psychoanalyst on the basis of his sexual orientation. Freud also wrote with great compassion to an American woman whose son was homosexual,[11] stating that, although homosexuality was no advantage, it should not be classified as an illness, nor should it be cause of shame. Freud believed that there was a biological component predisposing the individual toward homosexuality, but he also felt that a number of possible resolutions of the oedipal conflict could lead just as easily to homosexuality as to heterosexuality.[12]

Lewes and others (for example, Isay) have pointed out that much of the research on homosexuality has been based on people who were already in treatment, and that psychoanalysis has traditionally not paid adequate attention to those homosexuals who are functioning well. As is so often the case, many of Freud's followers have tended to be stricter than the master. Several generations of analysts and other mental health professionals have been generally judgmental about their homosexual patients, thus reinforcing the negative self-image already placed on them by society. A model of pathology has prevailed in which homosexuality has been viewed as an illness to be cured, even if much of the evidence has clearly indicated that this "disease" does not respond to treatment.

In the early sixties, discussions on homosexuality became more broad-based and were not confined to the psychoanalytic community. In June 1969, at a gay bar in New York City's Greenwich Village, homosexuals stood up en masse to protest police harassment for the first time. This event came to be known as the *Stonewall riots.*

In 1973, the American Psychiatric Association voted to delete homosexuality from the official list of psychiatric disorders: Homosexuality was no longer to be defined as a pathological condition. More recently several of the liberal wings among the major religious denominations have begun to both recognize and ordain openly gay and lesbian clergy. Although these decisions continue to be viewed as controversial, they nonetheless mark a significant milestone in the history of homosexuality.

Chapter 8

Gay Fathers and Lesbian Mothers

I started to get this baby hunger.
I just needed to have a child.
Lesbian Single Mother Who Was Artificially Inseminated

I always knew I wanted to be a father.
Single Gay Adoptive Father

Although there have probably always been "closet" homosexual parents, lesbian and gay parenting as a movement probably started sometime in the early 1970s. Even prior to that period, as well as before the ready availability of sperm banks, some lesbian women were already inseminating themselves, and growing numbers of people, both married and single, were starting to "come out of the closet."

As Stanley said, in one of the interviews referred to in the preceding chapter:

> Most men completely suppressed their gayness and got married thinking they were straight. Some of them were not even conscious they were gay until they were in their thirties. In the fifties, you were a fruit, a faggot,

someone society looked down on. Who would want to be identified with that?

SINGLE PARENTS BY DIVORCE

Most of the divorced homosexual parents I have met have indicated that, although their homosexuality contributed to the breakdown of the marriage, it was not necessarily the primary cause. One man told me that, when he finally admitted to his wife that he had been having periodic homosexual "excursions," she asked him to stop but did not want him to leave. He, on the other hand, felt that the marriage had little that was worthwhile to hold onto. Whereas many of the men felt that their wives had known on some level about their gay "tendencies" even before marriage, it is not clear if this was also the case with men married to lesbian women.

Stanley and his ex-wife reached a mutual agreement to share custody of their children. In Charlene's case, a custody battle ensued. Her first lawyer was very negative once he found out she was gay:

> My whole concept of myself was being buffeted around by how other people reacted, and the question the court kept asking was "When are you going to get remarried?"

She finally found herself another lawyer and was awarded custody, but without the court's ever knowing that she was gay. For others, the process was not always so straightforward.

When disputes arise over custody, the courts are required to determine custody and visitation rights based on the "best interest of the child." Many courts find the parent's sexual orientation relevant in determining the child's best interests and frequently deny custody to a gay or lesbian parent based on sexual orientation alone. Ten states expressly reject homosexuality as grounds for finding a person to be an unfit parent. When the gay parent is not the one awarded custody, limitations are often placed on visitation rights. When that parent is living with a partner, a common restriction is not allowing the partner to be present while the child is visiting.[1]

In a major first-time decision in 1973, a Michigan court awarded child custody to two lesbian mothers.[2] Although the courts are able to limit visitation, they have never been known to completely deny a child the right to a parent solely on the basis of sexual orientation.

Limitations on custody or visitation rights are usually based on one or more of the following rationales: (1) fear that the child will be harassed or ostracized; (2) fear that the child may become gay or lesbian; (3) fear of harm to the child's moral well-being; (4) fear that the child will be sexually molested; and (5) compliance with the state's sodomy statutes.[3] These rationales are currently being challenged.

The *Harvard Law Review* of 1990[4] stated that none of these rationales is sufficiently related to the child's best interests, nor are they supported by evidence. The *Review* further pointed out the following: Only one case presented with actual evidence of harassment has been presented in court; children of gays and lesbians have not been found to become homosexual any more often than children of heterosexuals; the judge's own view of moral well-being may not be consistent with what is in the child's best interest; child molesters are usually heterosexual men; and it is not statutorily permissible to base a custody or visitation decision on a sodomy statute, and, in any case, these statutes have been rescinded in half of the states.

Gay parental rights are currently being fought in the courts by organizations such as Lambda (Legal Defense and Education Fund, Inc.), the Lesbian Rights Project, and the Gay and Lesbian Parents Coalition International. Roberta Achtenberg, a chief proponent of gay and lesbian parental rights, states that there is no such thing as a homosexual personality and that homosexuals are no more likely to be neurotic, unhappy, or maladjusted than heterosexuals.

RESEARCH ON CHILDREN AND PARENTS

Research on gay fathers is limited, and rather more has been written about lesbian mothers and their children. The reason for this is that, in spite of current legal restrictions, it is still more common for mothers to get custody, regardless of sexual orientation. A brief survey of the literature illustrates some of the above points.

Prejudice against those not conforming to the norms of society is nothing new, and the children of gay parents have to deal not only with these issues, but also with their own reactions to their parents' lifestyle. Gay families usually choose to live in cities or neighborhoods that are tolerant of differences, and they select carefully which of their friends or acquaintances they feel they can safely come out to. Often, but not always, the choice is made to socialize primarily with other gay families. Although this protects them to some degree from being exposed to homophobia, it places limitations on the children, who, like the parents, live in a predominantly heterosexual world.

The lesbian mother frequently feels guilty about being gay, especially with regard to how it may adversely affect her children. However, her degree of comfort and self-confidence and how she views herself are usually reflected in how well her children are able to deal with homophobia. Often, these children become very sensitized to inequality and prejudice and, if confronted with negative reactions to their mother's homosexuality, handle it by viewing the people who have them as bigots and wish to have nothing to do with them. One study that measured children's perception of their own popularity with their peers[5] found no differences between the scores of children of lesbian mothers and those of a matched group of children of heterosexual mothers.

A number of studies have also examined the development of sexual orientation in the children of gay parents. Previous studies had suggested that boys who are separated from their fathers when very young are at risk of failing to develop a strong sense of masculine identity, regardless of the sexual orientation of the mother. However, studies on children of gay parents have generally not found any greater incidence of cross-gender identification than in the children of straight parents. One study that looked at children living in sexually atypical households—namely, gay and transvestite homes—found a clear preference for play, clothing, and toys traditionally associated with the child's own gender. The children in this study who were old enough to be sexually developed (their ages ranged from three to twenty) were all found to be heterosexual.[6]

Another study examined twenty latency-aged children living with their lesbian mothers and used a control group of matched children who were living with single heterosexual mothers.[7] The examiners used several different measures, which included meeting with the mothers separately and observing the children at play. The examiners, all child psychiatrists or psychologists, had no prior knowledge of the sexual orientation of the mothers. They found no differences in gender development between the children in the two groups. Furthermore, the examiners were unable to identify which mothers were gay, or which children were the children of lesbian mothers.

Although another study found that daughters of lesbian women tended to be less traditionally feminine than girls who had heterosexual mothers, they were not seen as being overtly masculine either.[8]

These findings suggest that children of gay and lesbian parents may be more similar to than different from children of heterosexual parents, especially when compared to families where there is no father in the home. One study found that the children of lesbian women who had been divorced were far more upset by the divorce than by their mothers' sexual orientation.[9] Many researchers suggest that the quality of the parenting is a far more important factor than the parent's sexual orientation in determining how well adjusted a child grows up to be. This observation might, of course, equally be applied to all children.

Nonetheless, children of gay parents are confronted with a unique set of problems. Essentially, they must deal with societal responses as well as their own responses and reactions. Typically, the most difficult periods are around the age of six or seven and early adolescence. In an interview, Barbara Rothberg, a family therapist who specializes in working with gay families, stresses the importance of being open about one's sexual orientation with one's children, rather than hiding it:

> Parents sometimes feel guilty and try to hide their gayness. But children will be angry, anyway, because they often don't like the lifestyle. Kids get more furious when they find out later. The worst period for disclosure is high school, when sexuality starts budding, but adolescence is the worst period for a child anyway. One commonly sees anger, embarrassment, direct questions, and sometimes acting out. The kids are usually conflicted that their parent is not "normal," because kids want to be like everyone else.

Dr. Rothberg stresses the need for the parent to allow the children to express their negative feelings about the parents being gay or lesbian, and to let them know that it is all right for them not to like it, and to wish that their parent were "normal."

Children typically have a tremendous amount of ambivalence about disclosing to their friends that a parent is gay. Reactions can range from "You're ruining my life" to "I'm proud of you, and if other kids don't like it, I don't want them to be my friends." Teenage girls usually express more anger than boys when they have a lesbian mother, whereas boys are able to put distance between themselves and their mothers. Two important determinants of how children cope with parental homosexuality are how secure the parents are in their sexual identity and the parental role and how much of a support system is available.[11]

CHARLENE grew up in a religious family, one of three children. Her mother was a difficult, undemonstrative woman, and she felt closer to her father, who was more available to her. When she first acknowledged to herself that she was a lesbian, she told her siblings, who were accepting. She didn't tell her parents until a few years ago, and her mother wouldn't speak to her for over six months. She feels that her family is only marginally there for her. Charlene is, however, very connected with many in the gay and lesbian community, from which she derives a great deal of support:

Most people have a biological concept of family and are not as familiar with the concept of a family of choice. I have a family by choice.

Although she is on her own now, after she left her husband she and her son, Derek, moved in with Leah and her two children, with whom she lived for several years. Although they are now apart, they are still very good friends:

We were very open with the children. We told them that there were different types of love, that your mom can love you, and your dad can love you, and there are different kinds of families. Some families just have a daddy, some have two mommies and some have two daddies.

Although Lance is now pretty open and relaxed, he went through a couple of difficult periods growing up. The first occurred when he was about eight, when his father disappeared. He started acting out and his grades dropped.

I was very concerned. It was very hard on me because I was feeling very guilty. I was saying, "Maybe I shouldn't be gay. Maybe I should give up this life." I thought about going out and dating men and finding a husband for my son's sake. There were problems about his own self-worth and identity.

Charlene went to a therapist, who told her that Lance was trying to connect himself to a male person in his life. Not having a particular man in her life, Charlene made an effort to have her own father establish a closer bond with Lance and eventually, the crisis passed—except for once, when he was thirteen.

He gave it to me, told me how he hated the fact that I was a lesbian and why couldn't I be like everyone else. On the one hand, I was cheering him on because I knew it had to come out, but I was upset. But he put his arm around me and said, "Mom, relax. You know I love you." Now we have a pretty solid relationship.

Charlene is selective about with whom she shares her sexual orientation, choosing to tell only those people she thinks will understand. Lance, also, only recently told a close friend that his mother is gay. Charlene feels that this was a great breakthrough for him. For a while, he didn't bring friends home because he felt uncomfortable, especially when she was living with Leah.

Charlene would rather be in a relationship than be single and feels this is true of most gay women. But dating can be difficult when you have a child, and she refuses to date someone who does not accept her son.

People who haven't lived with children or had children can get upset by the fact that they are not the primary person in my life. It's not that you don't love your lover, but the bond that exists between parent and child is different. I don't consider my lover my responsibility, but being a parent is a full-time job. I'm still responsible to help him continue growing.

Once, when Lance was younger, he asked his mother, a prolific reader, why she read only books written by women. "Don't you like men?" he asked. "If not, maybe you don't like me?"

I like men, I really do. There are lesbians who hate men, but it's a stereotype that doesn't always fit. The reality is heterosexual women hate men much more than any lesbian woman because they've been abused by men. Also, it's true that some lesbians are antichildren, but there are also heterosexual women who are anti-children. Unfortunately, some of them have children.

I asked if Charlene had any feelings about what Lance's sexual orientation will be:

Being gay is a hard life to choose. I would support him in whatever decision he makes. I would have chosen to be straight, but now I would not. There are more of us in the mainstream who are more out and more secure. People who are homosexual have regular jobs and pay taxes and watch their children and buy homes and work and live in Middle America. I am very happy now and much more secure, and my son is one loving and caring human being.

Gay men who first became open about their homosexuality after, rather than before, they became fathers usually experience more ambivalence in integrating the role of parent into their gay identity. As a result, gay fathers usually have more difficulty than lesbian women in disclosing their gay identity to their children.[11]

STANLEY waited three years before he told his children that he was gay:

It was a process. First, they had no contact with my gay friends; then, I started bringing them home. I heard of a gay fathers' support group, which I joined, but I was horrified to think of bringing the kids to any of their activities. I eventually did, though. Then, when I met Henry, I told them I was gay. The recommendation is that the earlier you tell them the better, but I wasn't sure. I had to say the word *gay* to them, but they said they already knew. I started crying, because it was such a relief to have told them.

I asked Stanley how he thinks the kids dealt with this:

Actually, the kids were very supportive of me, especially Paul. But who knows? The future will tell. We've always had a good relationship, and they seem to be well adjusted. They both have lots of friends and are doing well. As they were growing up, the house was always full of children coming and going. They never seemed to have any difficulty in introducing either me or Henry to their friends. The children did get some homophobia, though, from their mother, but that didn't seem to last long. Henry lived with us for about five years. He didn't have any children of his own but got pretty involved with my kids. We became a very standard household. We went on vacations together, to the movies, restaurants. We did all the things normal families do.

Shortly after his relationship with Henry broke up, Stanley started to date again. Stanley was disappointed that the relationship had ended, but Henry seemed ready to leave. Henry does, however, continue to stay in touch with the children:

Paul was by this time beginning to date, and he was dating girls while I was dating men. My ex-wife was actually kind of shocked that I was introducing my dates to the kids. She said to me, "You mean you actually bring them to the house for dinner?" I would never actually do that unless it was serious. I told her, "This is my life. I accept their life. They have to accept mine." They were fine with it, except they were concerned that I shouldn't get sick.

As his daughter, Linda, started moving into adolescence, she decided to go and live full time with her mother for a while, because she said the house was becoming too unstable. She was also beginning to have a hard time dealing with her father's homosexuality:

She was very angry with me, and we had it out one day. I told her I had loved her mother when we got married, and that I still like other ladies, but that this is something that is determined when you are born that you have no control over, and that she shouldn't feel bad. She was an adolescent and I thought that what she was doing was age-appropriate. It seemed to clear the air, and the following year, Linda asked if she could come back to live with me. She's been with me ever since, and things seem to be going fine.

Stanley is one of two children, whose parents came from a working-class background. He describes his parents' marriage as having been somewhat joyless. Although affection was shown to the children, who were the common denominator in the marriage, the parents seemed to have little else in common with each other. Stanley's father died shortly after Stanley came out and seemed to accept Stanley's homosexuality. His mother, in contrast, still cannot:

She has a terrible time dealing with it. I have tried to help her overcome it, but she cannot. She was very attached to Henry but would not let me bring him with me to visit her unless he came with a woman friend. She still hasn't told any of her friends. I would still like her approval.

His sister is married with two children:

She is very traditional, and it's kind of hard for her to accept me—we don't see much of each other.

I asked Stanley what he felt were the pluses and minuses of being a single parent:

I was the only man I knew taking care of his kids—don't forget it was the seventies. I would be picking them up from play dates and birthday parties with a bunch of other mothers. They were usually very nice and supportive, but it was hard to manage and run a job at the same time. I had a friend in the building, a divorced woman with two kids the same ages as mine—we were very close. It just happened, but I was conscious of the need to have a female role model around for them. I think kids mature faster when their parents are single. I think you share more and connect more when no spouse is around, so you have a chance to have a better relationship—not always, but it can happen.

On the surface the most difficult thing is the time factor, but the emotional commitment a father has to his children is something that someone who doesn't share that blood relation cannot fathom, and they interpret that emotional connection as putting them second. Some lovers don't want to get involved with the kids and wind up feeling like the wicked stepmother. I think it's harder for some gay men to be involved with a man who has children because their frame of reference has been themselves so much. Gay single men can afford to be self-absorbed, so that this can be a problem when it comes to dating.

Those of us who have been married and had kids have always lived in a family setup. It was fine for me to be involved with my kids. I did a good job because I wanted to. With a little luck, I seem to have raised happy, well-adjusted kids. We have our difficulties, but we are extremely close and we really care about each other.

SINGLE PARENTS BY ADOPTION

For the first time in history, people who are openly living as gays and lesbians are planning to have children. One lesbian mother perhaps reflected the view of many:

> There is no such thing as an accidental pregnancy when you are gay. Having a child is based on a deliberate decision, usually after much thought and soul searching. Gays who decide to become parents are faced with so many potential problems in terms of dealing with society

that they have to be very serious about wanting to become parents.

Many of the current legal restrictions have been challenged, and many more gays and lesbians are now becoming foster as well as adoptive parents. Approximately ten states have rejected presumptions against awarding custody to gay and lesbian parents on the basis of their sexual orientation alone. Florida and New Hampshire are now the only two states that specifically prohibit adoptions by homosexuals. New Hampshire also prohibits the placement of foster children in homosexual households, and Massachusetts has regulations intended to prevent gays and lesbians from becoming foster parents. Although most other states subtly discourage homosexuals from becoming adoptive or foster parents, it is not uncommon for agencies to make such placements, either because they are unaware that the applicant is gay, or because they judge the applicant to be capable of providing a good adoptive home. Such decisions are also influenced by how a particular judge may interpret the state's statutes.[13]

When seeking to adopt a child through a private agency, a potential parent does not usually offer information about her or his sexual orientation. Because this information is not generally directly asked for, the agency or caseworker may not know that the applicant is gay or may simply choose to ignore it.

JOHN first heard about the adoption agency where he got Jeffrey through an acquaintance, who told him about an agency in the Midwest that was sympathetic to singles wanting to adopt. He did not know, however, how sympathetic they were to gays. He did not tell them he was homosexual, but he suspects the social worker might have guessed:

If they know you're gay, they're supposed to tell the agency, but it's a bit fuzzy. It really often depends on the individual social worker you get and how understanding he or she is to gays wanting to adopt. This one seemed sympathetic.

After making the initial telephone call to the agency, John was told that he would be placed on a waiting list. Several weeks later, a social worker visited him to do a home study, which consisted of an inspection of his home and where the baby would sleep, as well as a fairly extensive interview. He was asked numerous questions about his background and education, why he wanted to become a parent, how he planned to take care of the child, and what his views were on child rearing. The following month, he received a call saying there was a woman due to give birth in a few months and was he interested:

I got phenomenally excited and told them yes. I had no preference for a boy or a girl. I thought it might be easier to raise a boy, but I would have taken whatever they offered.

Three months later, he drove to the airport to meet his new son, three-week-old Jeffrey, who was being flown in accompanied by the social worker. John was ecstatic:

The most shocking thing was that the social worker came home with me and then left. It was me and him. It was a little overwhelming—this little baby was totally dependent on me. But I thought to myself, "Babies have survived throughout the centuries, and I've been changing my nephews' and nieces' diapers and been around babies for years, so I will manage." The hardest part was getting up in the middle of the night. It was a drag getting up and being tired. The first time I bathed him, I was a bit nervous, but I didn't drown him. I had spoken to the pediatrician two weeks before Jeffrey came, and I had a variety of different people to call on—my mother, sister-in-law, family, friends. Knowing I had that support was very important.

John took six weeks off from work when Jeffrey arrived

and now works parttime in order to care for him. John has regular baby-sitters when he is running his business.

The whole procedure ended up costing John about seventeen thousand dollars. Although this sum is relatively high, costs vary enormously and depend on factors such as prenatal expenses for the mother and ethnic background. John says:

If you want a blond, blue-eyed child, you will often end up paying more and waiting longer than for, say, a black or Hispanic child.

When they first learned that he was going to adopt, John's parents were none too thrilled:

The family was not so comfortable. My parents asked me, "How can you bring a child into this crazy lifestyle?" But now, they love him, and they love being grandparents.

I asked what other kinds of reactions he has had:

It's not that people are against it. Rather, they don't understand it. People ask me, "Why would you want to be a father?" I know a lot of gay and lesbian people who would like to have children, and some of them are vicariously living through my being a father. Being gay does not mean not wanting children. I've always really liked kids, and I love having a child.

John does have concerns, however:

He will always know he is adopted, and he will always know his father's gay. I sent baby pictures to the biological mother and when he is eighteen, he can know who his biological parents are if he wants to. It may be a source of difficulty when he finds out his father is gay. He also may have problems with classmates and teachers. I expect to encounter homophobia, which he may get stuck in the middle of, but the onus is on me to make sure I do enough priming and prepping. As he questions his own sexuality, hopefully I will have raised him to be comfortable not to feel pressured to be like me. My hope is that he will grow up to be an outrageously open-minded, well-rounded straight man. That's my picture.

I asked, "What if he turns out to be gay?"

I think he will be extremely lucky in the sense of having a gay father.

I asked what had been John's biggest support:

Other gay and lesbian friends who were parents. More than half my friends are gay, but my world is very heterogeneous. There are a lot more support groups now for parents who are gay, and they have been very important. If they weren't around, I don't think I would have got this far. I don't know if I would have been a parent today. I've also got reinvolved in my church and had Jeffrey christened. I have such good memories of church as a child. I figured Jeff should have that experience, too.

According to the Gay and Lesbian Parents' Coalition International, as of 1992, there were well over a hundred formally registered groups in the United States and Canada and their number is growing rapidly. These groups generally offer social and recreational activities for both children and their parents. Such activities help people to feel less isolated in the community as well as provide the children with the opportunity to meet other families similar to their own. Besides social activities, many such groups also offer educational programs and act as advocates for the rights of gay parents.

I asked John what he found to be the greatest difficulties in being a single parent:

The most difficult thing has been doing the daily chores. Also, I don't want to short-change Jeffrey on time. I don't think I'm so different from any other single parent. I'm very much the nurturer, and I prefer being a single parent. The most important factor is that he's my child and only my child. I see couples, straight and gay, disagreeing about certain things.

Here it's very consistent, one person making the rules. I feel as if it works wonderfully.

One of the most difficult things about being a single parent is getting into a new relationship. I was in a couple of long-term relationships, but neither of them wanted children. Before Jeffrey, my picture of a relationship was distinct. We were going to live together, travel together, do things together, but now I am not so clear how a relationship would work out.

My own parents had an alright marriage. There were loving moments, but I wish they had been a little bit more affectionate with each other. They didn't really show that much affection in front of us. I was very close to my mother, but she was not very demonstrative toward us children. She never hugged or kissed us without our instigating it, as I remember. I would like Jeffrey to see me interact in a one-to-one relationship, but not similar to my upbringing of not seeing much affection.

At one point during our interview, while Jeffrey was sitting on my lap and playing, he started to fidget and cry. He seemed sleepy, and John said it was getting close to naptime. I tried to comfort Jeffrey, but he would not have it and, instead, slid off my lap and ran to his daddy. John lifted him up, looking thoughtful:

I've noticed that when he is cranky, he relates better to men than to women. I worry a lot about female role models. I am concerned about his interactions with women as he gets older, because he's not seeing me have a lot of them. I haven't planned to have one special woman in his life, but I do notice that we have a lot of women in our lives. But I think I will handle it as far as relationships go, because a lot of the interpersonal part of it is the same.

I asked what changes John anticipates in the future:

I think society is changing, but more because of the work the gay and lesbian community is doing in educating people.

They are being confronted, and their homophobia is being knocked down by force!

John is in the process of planning to adopt a second child.

SINGLE PARENTS BY ARTIFICIAL INSEMINATION

Following World War II, major advances in medicine, particularly in the area of infertility, have resulted in a significant increase in the numbers of children conceived through artificial insemination. In a 1987 survey, it was estimated that 172,000 women had undertaken artificial insemination in the period 1986–1987 alone.[13] Although it is relatively simple to arrange to be artificially inseminated, either through personal contact, a private physician, or a sperm bank, some states have statutes that prohibit the provision of artificial insemination to unmarried women. In addition, although many physicians will agree to artificially inseminate a woman, regardless of her marital status or sexual orientation, others refuse to do this for unmarried or lesbian women because of their own moral or religious beliefs. Currently, only two sperm banks in the country openly offer such services to lesbian women: the Feminist Women's Health Center in Atlanta, Georgia, and the Sperm Bank of California, with two locations in Northern California.

When large numbers of lesbian women first started being artificially inseminated in the sixties, donor anonymity was usually the preferred method, because many feared the possibility of facing a child custody suit. This no longer is a factor, as those states having statutes related to artificial insemination have eliminated donor paternity in the case of unmarried women.[14] Many lesbian women were also making a political statement, no doubt influenced by the women's movement as well as gay liberation, in not wishing to have any involvement with a biological father.

There is a much greater awareness today of the possible effects on children who have no knowledge of their biological roots, whether because of adoption or artificial insemination. Far more people now hold the view that the use of an unknown donor deprives children of half their heritage. In a poignant article, a forty-two-year-old woman who was conceived through anonymous artificial insemination, wrote that she was never quite able to forgive her parents for having kept the details of her conception a secret from her.[15] Although she is but one example, many more lesbian women are now deciding to inseminate with the option that information regarding the sperm donor be made available to the child.

The sperm bank SARA went to said they would burn the records before opening them up:

At the time, I didn't care, but now I feel a sadness for Justin because, if he wants to know, I think it should be his right.

Sara was inseminated in her doctor's office:

They took the sperm out of the freezer, and five minutes later it was ready. He inserted it with a straw, three days in a row. I planned to do this on my own, but hoped to find a woman to do it with me. But the biological clock was ticking, and I had always wanted a child.

Justin asked when he was two-and-three-quarters, "Where is my daddy?" I said, "Some families don't have daddies," and that was it. A few months later, he said, "I miss my daddy. Where is my daddy?" And so I repeated what I'd said the first time, but he didn't let it go this time: "Does my daddy live far away? Can we call him? Can we go see him?" I explained that I never knew his father, and that I wanted him so badly that I went to a doctor's office and the doctor helped me make Justin.

I felt terrible that day; it got me in the depths. We were in a neighbor's home, and the children greeted their father, and after that, Justin said, "I want a father." It was the first time he really sounded sad, almost started to cry: "I want a daddy to play with." I said, "But you have me to play with, and I can't give you a daddy."

Since then I have seen him handle it well. A kid said, "What's your daddy's name?" and he said very casually, "I don't have a daddy."

He's been exposed to different families socially—two mothers, two fathers, and mixed—and feels it's OK. But he's been challenged at school and came back to me and said that. I told him that most people marry someone of the opposite sex and don't know about other families.

Sara has come out in most places about being lesbian, but hesitates to come out to the parents of Justin's playmates for fear he will suffer the consequences:

Most of my social life is within the gay community. But it's kind of split. I am friends with the mothers of Justin's playmates at school, but I am not out to them. I love to chat with mothers on the park bench, but I have to conceal a major part of myself from them for fear of being rejected.

We are living in a norm that is heterosexual. While we are living alone, why should he be exposed to fighting a lesbian battle? In a way, it's easier to be invisible when you are a single mother. In other words, if I can pass, I leave it alone.

On the weekends we do a lot with Center Kids and they're wonderful. I also have a big family, lots of cousins and friends who are straight. I didn't lose any of my friends when I came out, but I did lose one when I became a mother. She was straight and was very uncomfortable with infants.

Center Kids is a New York City-based group that was created by and for families headed by lesbians and gay men. It was established in the summer of 1988 by a handful of parents and within four years had a mailing list of over 1300 households spanning New York City's five boroughs as well as Westchester and New Jersey. More than half the members are already parents and it is estimated that 10 to 15 percent of these are single parents. The other 50 percent is composed of people who are thinking or waiting or applying to become parents. The group offers social events geared to children and gives them an opportunity to learn that other children are living with lesbian and gay parents. Center Kids offers a range of educational resources and also advocates for the rights of its members.

Sara says:

When I first told my parents I was gay, they thought I was going through one of my intellectual phases—until I started taking lovers. Then they accepted it.

My mother was emotionally limited. No hugs and kisses, the very opposite of my father. My father seemed to be strong, and my mother seemed to be very wishy-washy. I didn't want to be like her. I identified with my father much more. I think there are family dynamics at the base of why I decided to be with women, and I don't rule out the possibility of being with a man. Men still turn me on, but it's more comfortable when I am with a woman.

I asked Sara what the positives are of being a single mother:

I would have preferred to have done it with a partner. I am a mother by choice, but not single by choice. I think that's the case with most single parents. One of the plusses is I don't have to listen to someone's opposite opinion and I can do what I want. But there is no one to hand him over to if he gets to me, no backup. I have to make all the decisions myself: which school he should go to, which doctor. We are alone together more than I would like, because as soon as another caretaking person is around, I relax. There is a bumper, someone else for him to go to. The finances are also sometimes difficult.

I asked what she wishes for Justin:

I just hope whatever he does will be less stressful and guilt-ridden. For me it would be all right if he wanted to be with a man, but if he were swishy, I would be very upset. The very outward feminine qualities of some men bother me. But I will give him constant backup and support.

Last year Sara and Justin marched in the Gay Pride parade in New York City:

There were hundreds of people marching who were as regular-looking as the people who were watching. But the television news coverage only showed the floats showing something about AIDS and the ones that were the weirdest, way out. They didn't show the children and the education groups, and they didn't show the church groups and the family groups, and so they're not showing the most normal people, whom the people who are watching could identify with. They only showed crazies.

One of the questions I have asked parents is, what they would like this book to say. John's response speaks for itself and perhaps also speaks for others:

I would hope that people who read this book would see that people who are gay and lesbian are loving their children and raising them just the way anyone else does. And that they are doing a good job being parents. That's what I hope.

As the visibility of gays and lesbians is growing and more and more are openly entering into the mainstream of society, it is inevitable that many will wish to assume roles and responsibilities not previously available to them. When the demarcation line between who was gay and who was straight was more easily identifiable, when many gays both looked and behaved differently, as well as kept largely to specified professions, perhaps many straight people found it easier to tolerate them, on the one hand, while rejecting them, on the other.

As these lines have become less clearly apparent, is it possible that yet another set of problems has been introduced? Michel Foucault answered the question this way:

> [The] common fear [is] that gays will develop relationships that are intense and satisfying, even though they do not all conform to the ideas of relationships held by others. The prospect that gays will create as yet unforeseen kinds of relationships, many people cannot tolerate.

Chapter 9

Families around the World

Teems of times and happy returns. The seim anew.
Ordovico or Viricordo. Anna was, Livia is,
Plurabelle's to be.

Finnegans Wake

As both single-parent families and the absence of marriage have come to be viewed as more socially acceptable in the 1980s and 1990s, we may well ask what further changes can be anticipated. Certainly, such questions are not unique to the United States. Perhaps, by looking at family trends in other industrialized societies, we may gain some further insight into what the family may look like by the year 2000.

SWEDEN

The changes in family patterning in Sweden most epitomize the trends we have been witnessing in recent decades. One of the most egalitarian countries in the world, Sweden moved from being a paternalistic to being an egalitarian society at the turn of the century. Since that time, the church, which is primarily Lutheran, has had little impact in prescribing family values.

With its deemphasis on marriage, Sweden has moved further away from the nuclear family than any other industrialized society today. Before the mid-1960s, Sweden had shown relatively little difference in its marital patterns from other European countries. At that time, marriage rates began to decrease sharply, dropping 40 percent over seven or eight years. By 1980, Sweden's marriage rate (per 1,000 women aged twenty-five to twenty-nine) was 78, compared to 99 in Denmark, 109 in Japan, 117 in France, 127 in the United States, and 168 in England and Wales.[1] The Swedish marriage rate for that same group of women was 73.2 in 1990.[2]

Sweden has not only the lowest marriage rate in the industrialized world, but also the highest number of unmarried couples who live together. Approximately 25 percent of couples who are living together are not married, compared to 2.5 percent in Great Britain and 5 percent in the United States. Moreover, nearly half of all births in Sweden take place outside of marriage. This is a very much accepted norm in Swedish society, both legally and socially, and is viewed as virtually comparable to marriage. When marriage does occur, it often takes place upon the arrival of children. However, even then, marriage is by no means looked on as a necessity. Illegitimacy as a legal concept was legislatively removed in the early 1970s, and all children are considered equal within the law.[3]

Given these facts, it is surprising that Sweden has a very high rate of divorce, and an even higher rate of breakup within cohabiting couples. Moreover, it is estimated that Sweden has the highest rate of family breakups in the industrialized world.[4] Because the Swedes are free to try different lifestyles unimpeded by social constraints, one would imagine that, once a choice was finally made to marry, these unions would be long-lasting. This does not, however, appear to be the case.

As would be expected, in addition to having many unmarried couples living together with their children, Sweden also has a high number of single-parent families. In 1980, 18 percent of all Swedish households with children were single-parent families, compared to 17 percent of American white families and 52 percent of American black families.[5]

Attitudes toward homosexuality have also undergone considerable change in Sweden. In 1979, the Swedish National Board of Health and Welfare declassified homosexuality as a mental disturbance and in 1987, legal recognition was given to lesbian and gay relationships. Interestingly, Sweden permits gay and lesbian individuals (but not couples) to adopt children. While this does not mean that no discrimination against gays and lesbians exists in Sweden, the legal position stands in sharp contrast to countries such as Austria, where organizations advocating, promoting, or approving of homosexuality are prohibited, and Finland, where it is illegal to disseminate information about homosexuality.[6]

Even though there are no known Swedish statistics on single parents by choice, it is probable that a small number exist. Single mothers in general do not experience the same economic hardships often found in other countries, as Sweden provides an extensive array of child care programs. New parents are given a paid leave of absence, and single mothers are given first priority for places in state-run day-care centers.[7]

GREAT BRITAIN

The situation is very different in Great Britain (England, Scotland, and Wales), where more than one family in seven is headed by a lone parent, and children born outside marriage continue to be heavily censured. In France, where nearly a third of all children are born outside of marriage,[8] negative attitudes are even stronger. Divorce rates in England and Wales have reached record levels, comparable to those of the United States, and one marriage in three is expected to end in divorce.[9]

Great Britain is estimated to have the highest proportion of one-parent families and, with the exception of Portugal, the poorest publicly funded child care program in Europe. There are currently thought to be over one million such families in Great Britain, or one in seven of all families with dependent children, and there is a steady growth in the proportion of births taking place outside marriage.[10] Homosexual acts between consenting adult males have been legal in England and Wales since the 1967 Sexual Offences Act. However, Great Britain has more laws that discriminate against homosexuals than any other European country.[11] Although pressure groups are attempting to bring Great Britain more into line with the rest of Europe, the introduction in 1991 of a bill into the House of Commons seeking to further restrict homosexual activity suggests a move to the right, at least on the part of some in England.[12]

Two national British organizations represent one-parent families: the National Council for One Parent Families, founded in 1914, and Gingerbread, a self-help organization that has three hundred groups across the country. Each offers a range of services, which focus on the economic hardships that many of these parents face. The National Council also actively campaigns for the rights of single-parent families, including seeking to end discrimination against children born outside marriage.

Although there are no known British groups specifically geared to single parents by choice, and the above organizations purport to represent all single parents and their children, recent correspondence published in the Gingerbread newsletter suggests that there is a good deal of ambivalence regarding women who deliberately choose single motherhood, even within this organization.[13] Nonetheless, the numbers of older, unmarried women having children in Britain have reached unprecedented levels, a fact suggesting that inspite of the prevailing social sanctions women are increasingly making this choice. A book describing the experiences of these women in America and Holland, as well as in Britain, was published in England in 1985.[14]

ISRAEL

Israel is a country full of anomalies. Although non-Orthodox Jewish women are required to serve in the army, a seeming indication that Israel is a sexually egalitarian society, women are very much tied to the religious jurisdiction of the courts when it comes to matters dealing with marriage and divorce. Na'amat, the largest women's organization in Israel, estimates that some 8,000 women are *agunot,* or legally bound to their husbands because the husbands refuse to grant them a religious divorce.

Israel is a country with strong family values. Nevertheless, it has not been immune to the social changes sweeping much of Western society. The divorce rate, lower than that in most European countries, is, nevertheless, rising. Excluding the recent influx of immigrants from the former Russian states, divorce rates have doubled since the early 1980s, and approximately five thousand divorces are currently granted each year. As these figures continue to climb, it is predicted that, within the next fifteen to twenty years, one out of every four Israeli marriages will end in divorce,[15] which is comparable to current figures in Great Britain and the United States. Interestingly, it is estimated that, of the Russian families coming into the country, about 20 percent are single-parent families, which is about 11 percent higher than in the current Israeli population.[16]

Over 10 percent, or more than sixty thousand Israeli families, are headed by one parent, about five thousand of whom are estimated to be women who have deliberately chosen to become single mothers.[17] The numerous wars that Israel has faced over the years have resulted in a shortage of men, and many women have been unwilling to forgo motherhood because they were unable to find a husband. Children coming from these families are often faced with stigma and social sanctions. Mothers without Marriage (Emahot Lo Nisuot, or Elen for short), an organization that was established in 1982, seeks to gain a greater degree of both legal and social acceptance for these children and their families. As in its American counterpart, Single Mothers by Choice, many of the members are in their late thirties and early forties and come from professional or middle-class backgrounds. Mechad, an association for single-parent families run under the auspices of Na'amat, offers a variety of supportive services and also lobbies for legislative changes. In its view, the two-parent family can no longer be looked on as the only model, and that the single-parent family is merely another normative form of family life today.

Homosexuality is an abomination in the Jewish Bible. However, this severity must be viewed in its historical context; procreative sex was of primary importance for a minority group. In Israel, the lack of separation between religious and state authorities inevitably impedes any efforts made to gain rights for gays and lesbians. Nonetheless, attitudes toward homosexuality are undergoing some change. In 1988, the Knesset, Israel's parliament, repealed a law that had made homosexual sex between two consenting adults a criminal act. In 1983, the military dropped its ban on openly gay and lesbian enlistees, even though they are unable to advance to high rank.

Although recognizing the necessity for Israel to focus much of its energy on issues pertaining to national security and absorption of its many new immigrants, the gay community nonetheless feels that its needs have been given scant attention. A political group for gays and lesbians, the Society for the Protection of Personal Rights, was founded in 1975. Its approximately 250 members focus primarily on lobbying and public education programs. The gay community puts out two publications, *Maga'im* and *Netiv Nosaf*, and *Davar*, a national daily newspaper, publishes a weekly supplement that addresses gay and lesbian issues.

Chapter 10

W(h)ither the Family?

> Come mothers and fathers, throughout the land
> And don't criticize what you can't understand.
> Your sons and your daughters are beyond your command,
> Your old road is rapidly agin'
> Please get out of the new one if you can't lend your hand,
> For the times they are a'changin'.
>
> Bob Dylan

We have had the opportunity here to be privy to the lives of a special group of parents. Most of them, although subscribing to the view that the active presence of both a mother and a father is optimal for a child, have nonetheless chosen to be single parents. Moreover, many of them seem to be doing quite well and not very differently from some two-parent families.

The question of whether the family is in decline is being posed today by both professionals and laypersons alike. Certainly, the family as we have known it no longer represents the majority of American households, and similar shifts are also occurring in much of the rest of the Western world. Exactly how these changes will come to be viewed in future years remains to be seen.

In order to have a clearer understanding of what such

changes represent, it is important to recognize that the family
serves as a refractor of society, on which the numerous social
changes of recent decades have left their imprint. Not only
have various economic shifts led to the general demise of
the single-income household, but the growing democratization of society, affecting women in particular, has resulted in
the expansion of women's roles significantly beyond those of
Küche, Kirche, und Kinder. The impact of the various social
movements—the civil rights movement, the sexual revolution,
the women's movement, and the gay movement, to mention
only a few—has not, of course, affected the lives only of
women. We have become a nation increasingly tolerant of
diversity and difference, one that has made some marked
shifts away from the values of familism in favor of those of
individualism. On the other hand, we are currently witnessing
growing signs of conservatism in the land.

Change is a very complex matter, for both the individual
and the group. Human beings are very much creatures of
habit, who when confronted with new ideas, may be forced to
reexamine old belief systems that touch a basic and sometimes even a primitive core. When shifts in social patterning
first occur, they are viewed with suspicion because they are
seen as a potential threat to the status quo. They continue to
be viewed this way unless they succeed in either becoming
integrated into the currently existing social framework or
come to replace old norms. Most of the families described in
this book seem to be poised at this point of potential change.

Such a process of change usually occurs over a period of
many years. Our problem today is that we seem to have
reached a saturation point: societal changes have been emerging at such a rapid rate that we have not had time to sufficiently digest and absorb them. The result has been much
confusion. Of particular note here are changes in both the
definition and the role of the family.

An example is the mixed messages we are receiving regarding child-rearing practices in this country. On the one

hand, there is a greater recognition of the need for women to work outside the home, yet there are neither fiscal incentives to make it feasible for one parent to stay home to care for the children, nor is there sufficient quality child care available to enable women to remain in the work force.

Although a society is rarely static, clearly we are still in the midst of a long period of transition. At such a time, we can expect the emergence of many new definitions and family forms. As an example, a 1989 ruling concerning the New York City rent control laws defined a gay couple as a family.[1] In another instance, a Washington State judge recently allowed a lesbian woman to adopt her lover's baby, and a birth certificate was issued containing the names of two mothers.[2]

Although the families described in this book represent only a tiny fraction of the population, approximately one child in four now lives with a single parent, so that one-parent families have become a significant and real presence in our society. A great deal has already been written about families of divorce and what has been traditionally referred to as the unwed mother, but little has been written about single men and women who are opting to become parents.

It is too early to say whether these modes of parenting will come to be looked on as viable alternatives to the two-parent family, and thus new norms. Whatever the outcome, they represent yet another variation in the changing complexion of the American family. Although conclusions cannot be drawn before we have a greater understanding of how well the children have done, let us take a further look at some of the factors constituting social change. For a new or previously unacceptable practice to become accepted as a social norm, certain factors must be present. First, enough people must participate in that practice so that its impact is widely felt. Second, there must be a reevaluation of the attitudes and beliefs related to that practice. Finally, if such a practice is seen as reflecting current values of the society, it may well come to be adopted as a new norm.

An illustration is the changes that have occurred in attitudes toward premarital sex. Whereas intercourse before marriage was previously considered outside acceptable standards of behavior, this practice is now frequently taken for granted. Divorce, on the other hand, represents a norm that is still in a state of flux. Although divorce is rarely accompanied today by the same degree of stigma found in earlier periods, it has yet to become a social norm, although it may well be on the way. Similarly, although there are far more single-parent families today than in earlier periods, few people are advocating them as a norm.

As we can see, the presence of a growing trend is a necessary, but not a sufficient, impetus to change in social attitudes. If it were *sufficient,* we might well find homelessness and drug addiction becoming acceptable societal norms.

Clearly, single adults who have chosen to become parents represent a growing, although small, trend. Let us look at the two components of that trend—being single and being a parent—each of which has undergone changes of its own.

First, singlehood. Of the close to eighty million American adults who are now single, it is predicted that 10 percent will never marry. Even if many cohabit with a partner at some point in their lives, these figures are nevertheless mind-boggling. Moreover, a person who has never married can no longer be viewed as necessarily being a social isolate or as living an unsatisfying or incomplete life.

In a recent in-depth study of never-married men between the ages of forty and fifty, most were found to be extremely independent and self-reliant, and many to be leading very satisfying lives. They were, however, generally wary of relationships.[3] In a similar study, white women in their late thirties not only were seen as having positive self-images but were also found to be emotionally connected to others. Many had made important decisions in their lives that had not been organized around getting married. The study concluded that

never-married women were likely to be functioning better, ed-
ucationally as well as economically, than never-married men.[4]
    What about parenthood—and motherhood in particular?
Although the rate of childbirth has, in fact, been going up,
growing numbers of couples no longer view parenthood as
a necessary or inevitable factor in their lives. Traditionally,
women saw their identities to be very much bound up in the
roles of wife and mother, but these perceptions have changed,
and many women, and also men, now look on parenthood as
an option rather than a sociological imperative. As a result,
increasing numbers of couples are choosing to remain childless. Thus, we are, paradoxically, being faced with a new
social script in which some couples are choosing to remain
childless, and some singles are opting for parenthood.
    Even though a wave of conservatism is appearing in the
United States, a trend simultaneously emerging in other Western countries, we remain a society that has become increasingly tolerant of diversity and difference. To what extent the
emergence of these diverse families is a reflection of a greater
acceptance of nonconformity, and to what degree it may reflect the growing focus on individualism, is unclear. What is
apparent, however, is that, although marriage and parenthood
continue to be highly valued by most people, the link between
them has become unavoidably weakened.
    What about the children? Certainly, the parents who were
interviewed here were generally very aware of their situation and how it might impinge on the lives of their children.
They were extremely committed to their role as parents and
were trying to provide their children not only with additional
meaningful adult relationships, but also with other enriching
experiences. It is still too early to assess the full implications
for children being raised by single parents, and especially
how they may compare with children growing up in two-
parent families. No doubt, many studies will be done on these
children, particularly when a sufficient number of them have
reached adolescence or early adulthood. In the meantime, let

us take a look at single parenthood, from a psychological and sociological perspective.

PSYCHOLOGICAL PERSPECTIVE

The contribution of Freud to our understanding of early childhood and personality development has left an indelible mark on all subsequent thinking on these subjects. His oral, anal, and phallic phases of psychological development culminate with the Oedipus complex. According to oedipal theory, when the child reaches the age of about four or five, she or he develops strong feelings of libidinal attachment to the opposite-sex parent. At the same time, jealousy arises toward the same-sex parent, who is perceived as being the recipient of the opposite-sex parent's attention, and thus a rival. How the child resolves these unconscious conflicts was viewed by Freud as a major determinant of the development of personality and sexual identity, and as the basis for neurosis.

Although the Oedipus complex continues to be a focal point in psychodynamic theory, its meaning has been greatly modified by later theorists, for both Freudians and non-Freudians. To paraphrase Arnold Modell, describing the Oedipus complex today is a bit like shooting at a moving target.[5] Although many have retained the view that it is a universal phenomenon, some have questioned its central role in personality development, and others have questioned its validity altogether. As greater emphasis came to be placed on the earlier, preoedipal periods, greater attention was also given to the quality of the early nurturing relationships. Other factors, such as a child's physical and emotional constitution, the environment, and the role of other family members like the siblings also came to be recognized for their contribution to early child development.

From a psychodynamic perspective, the absence of a second parent invariably places a child at risk. The earlier such an absence is experienced, the greater an impact it is expected to have on a child's development. For example, during early infancy, at a time when the mother–child relationship is intensely close, the presence of a third person (presumably the father) is viewed as essential because it helps to dilute the intensity of this relationship, especially as the infant begins to move toward separation and individuation. The absence of a third person may result in the infant's having difficulties in negotiating separation–individuation and, instead, remaining inadequately separated and overly attached to the mother. From this perspective, later issues, such as achieving an "oedipal victory" in the absence of a rival, are, similarly, viewed as affecting sexual development adversely.

Of the surprisingly few studies in the psychological literature on children raised by one parent, most focus on children who have suffered the loss of an existing relationship with the parent, through either death or divorce. Moreover, these studies tend to deal with the loss of a father, which is certainly a more common occurrence than the loss of a mother.

Studies that have specifically addressed single-parent families from birth have usually dealt with families in which the parents were young, uneducated, and poor. There are no known studies of children who were raised from birth by a single parent without socioeconomic deprivation and without "actual" loss of a parent. How the dynamics differ in such circumstances can only be conjectured at this point.

Evidence from other cultures, such as the work of Margaret Mead and studies on Israeli kibbutz children, suggests that children can develop in a healthy fashion when many good "mothers" are available. Furthermore, in the study of fatherless children in wartime London, Anna Freud and Dorothy Burlingham concluded that, when no father is present, children who are at the oedipal phase create a father in fantasy.[6]

Other studies, nonetheless, have stressed the early importance of the father. Ernest Abelin found the presence of strong attachment behavior toward the father as early as nine months. In what he referred to as "early triangulation," he felt that children experience not only each parent separately, but also the parents' relationship with each other.[7] Abelin found children openly vying for attention from more than one person at a time as early as eighteen months. He did not see this behavior as motivated by jealousy, more typical of the oedipal stage, but rather as an attempt on the part of the child to unite the two parents.[8] In a similar vein, a study examining the Oedipus complex in women suggested that little girls do not turn away from their mothers during the oedipal period, but rather maintain close ties to them and, at the same time, develop a different quality of attachment to their fathers.[9]

In his emphasis on the child's need to have a "different" or "other" parent to turn to in addition to the mother, particularly during the period of beginning separation, Abelin suggested that this "parent" does not necessarily have to be the father:

> To be sure, the "other" is not only and not always the father. The child's earliest "social space" may differ greatly from one culture to another.[10]

Might one suggest that such "social space" may also differ within a given culture? For are we not witnessing major shifts in child-rearing practices within our own culture today? With increasing numbers of mothers, both married and single, entering the work force, many preschool-aged children are now being left in the care of persons other than the parent for large portions of the day. When a child is left with the same caregiver over an extended period of time, that person inevitably assumes some of the functions of the mother and consequently becomes an important figure in the child's internal as well as external life. Further, in the absence of a second parent, the caregiver assumes an even greater importance in that child's development that is undoubtedly played out within the context of the mother–caregiver–child triangulation. One wonders what must have happened in Freud's day to the children of Viennese society who were left almost exclusively in the care of nannies, and who had little contact with their mothers and even less with their fathers. Freud himself was a case in point.

SOCIOLOGICAL PERSPECTIVE

Sociologists note that key shifts in cultural values tend to occur in thirty-year cycles, or about once in every generation. There is also a tendency for values to shift back and forth between those of social bonds and individual choice.[11]

From the 1940s to the 1960s traditional family values were at an all-time high. The mid-1960s to the mid-1980s came to be characterized by their preoccupation with individualism, with values such as self-fulfillment and self-actualization gaining primacy. Not only was this a period of social ferment, but also a time that offered a sense of hope and emancipation to many minority and formerly subordinated groups. It was a time for experimentation, for turning away from the old and trying out the new. As one woman put it, "It was like walking into a candy store. You could try anything. You could have it all!" It was against such a backdrop that most of the parents interviewed for this book grew up.

There are some signs that the pendulum may be getting ready to swing back again. Even though the figures for marriage remain low and divorce figures are high, a move away from the values of individualism, particularly among the middle class, appears to be under way.

A number of factors influence such social shifts, notably the state of the economy. For example, many people are now staying married and trying to work things out because, unlike in previous decades, divorce in the 1990s is simply too expensive. Another major factor is the impact that AIDS and other sexually transmitted diseases have had on coupling patterns. When people are confronted with the possibility of economic distress or illness, social support systems come to assume a greater importance in their lives than the things that money can buy.

In addition, as women have come to feel increasingly accepted in the workplace, some have begun to question whether work satisfaction is a sufficient substitute for satisfaction in the home. Growing numbers of women, as well as men, are now pressing for extended maternity and paternity leave, as well as for the provision of more high-quality childcare facilities.

Finally, as the generation of baby boomers, about forty-five million in all, have reached adulthood, many of them have become parents:

> This is a huge generation. It is a generation that invented singlehood as a "lifestyle," that cohabited and delayed marriage and childbearing. But this generation has now settled down into family life.[12]

Among these people, some have settled down to family life while remaining single. Surely, by dint of size alone, this generation will have a significant impact on American society in the years to come.

David Popenoe suggests that the shift toward familism may well be aided by what he calls "the battered generation," namely, the children born during the divorce-prone years of the 1970s. Although the statistics may be against them, many of those whose parents divorced are focusing heavily on the values of a stable family life as they themselves are reaching adulthood.[13]

The family has, of course, always been highly valued, even in the 1970s. But although those on the political right, as well as much of Middle America, have always viewed the nuclear family as the only viable model, it is to the left of center that the greatest changes are taking place. Many of those who grow up in a time of great social unrest, when many of the traditional norms were in question, are now moving more toward family values, although not necessarily in conventional form. Whereas the conservative viewpoint looks upon becoming a single parent as an act of hubris, many liberals, including some of the more progressive branches of the major religious denominations, see choosing to take on the responsibility of child rearing as laudatory in any form.

These changes coincide with our no longer being able to view ourselves as a child-oriented society. The struggles that many groups have undergone in recent decades have inevitably, and perhaps unavoidably, led us to become a more adult-focused society. This change has certainly left its mark on the family. Many of the decisions made within the context of the family may ultimately have been in the best interests of the adult members, but often the children have been the losers.

Furthermore, children are spending less time with their parents because so many parents must now work, and at the same time, there is not enough affordable high-quality child care available. In spite of our being in an age of psychological enlightenment, which stresses the critical role of the early formative years, the needs of children are simply not considered a high priority in this country.

The practical concerns of child care remain a central issue facing the changing family today. Even the women's movement has not focused adequately on how to reconcile the problems of mothers who must work and yet care for their children: "Mainstream feminists have generally treated motherhood as something most women want to avoid."[14] The United States lags far behind many European countries in providing programs for working parents and their children, especially programs sensitive to early developmental needs. We seem, both literally and metaphorically, to be "throwing out the baby with the bathwater."

The changing role of the father has also had an impact.

As the numbers of one-parent families have grown, and continue to grow, men have increasingly become removed from family life. One striking example is to be seen within the black community, where the pattern of the matriarchal family is prevalent, particularly among the poor. Many children coming from these families have to contend not only with economic hardships, poor schools, and violence as a daily diet, but also with the absence of a viable black male role model. Twice as many working-age African-American males as whites are unemployed, and one out of every four between the ages of twenty-six and twenty-nine is in jail, on parole, or on probation.[15] These families are indeed being dealt a double blow. As for divorce, in all racial and ethnic groups, "a substantial and growing fraction of non-residential fathers spend little time with their children nor offer them much in the way of material or emotional support."[16]

Thus, although, according to our biopsychological script, the role of the father is essential, our contemporary cultural script tells another story. The man, once charged with being a good husband, father, and provider, is no longer seen as indispensable to meet these needs. Although men were never as dependent, as were women, in defining themselves according to their identity as spouse and parent, these were, nonetheless, roles that many men very much took for granted.

This is no longer the case. As men cannot be certain of gaining acceptance in these roles, and thereby achieving some sense of self-worth, many are backing away from the commitment to permanent relationships and seem to be looking elsewhere for fulfillment, be it in achievement in the marketplace, in making a lot of money, or in sexual or physical prowess.[17] The popularity of such books as Robert Bly's *Iron John* and Sam Keen's *Fire in the Belly* seem to be a reflection of some of the identity issues that men are currently facing, and we may well be witnessing the burgeoning of a men's movement.

The fact that a family may lack the presence of a father does not necessarily mean that men per se are not valued in that family. Nonetheless, one cannot avoid wondering what the implications are for the children, especially for boys, when this is the case.

The presence of both a strong support system and an emotionally and physically stable environment are of especial importance to single-parent families. Whether the support comes from the community, the extended family, or friends, it has a particular significance for a parent carrying the entire burden of raising a child alone. Single mothers have, in fact, been found to be very resourceful in establishing support networks for themselves and their children. Moreover, the presence of another interested and concerned individual may offer much-needed respite for a lone parent, as well as provide an important and meaningful relationship to the child. And if that third person is of the opposite sex, so much the better.[18]

Although we do not yet know enough about the experiences of children who were raised by single parents from birth, we do know that a stable home is a major determinant of how quickly children are able to adjust following a divorce. Children living in generally conflict-free homes following a divorce are not only likely to demonstrate relatively rapid improvements if their behavior had previously deteriorated in response to the parental tensions, but to compare favorably with children who are living in intact but conflictual households. Such behavioral improvements have been observed regardless of whether the children were living with their mother or their father.

In a recent study of behavioral problems in children of divorce, many of the problems were found to have existed well before the divorce. Many were attributable to the children's having been exposed to their parents' marital tensions and conflicts while the family was still living together.[19] One might say that, although it is important for a child to be living in an intact family with two parents, it is perhaps equally important that there be relative peace in the home.

In contrast to two-parent families, different patterns in the hierarchical chain of command are often seen when just one parent is present. It is not unusual for children living with a single parent to be included in the important decision-making and household duties much earlier than usual. As a result, these children often develop a different kind of relationship with their parent, one that is more of a partnership, although a junior partnership. Because of the additional responsibilities carried by the single parent, this partnership is sometimes encouraged, and as a result, the children often grow up a little faster.

Although this share in family responsibility is positive for some children, it may place too large a burden on others, especially when they also become confidantes of their parents. In such cases, the children may become overly focused on the parent, at the expense of their own emotional needs. Some of these children may give the impression of being overly precocious and mature, especially if that is what they sense the parent wants of them, but while masking their own unmet developmental needs.[20]

CONCLUSIONS

We will now see what general conclusions may be drawn from our interviews with single parents. As most of the people we have met have been women, we will first look at them.

The following comments apply primarily to the women described in Chapters 2 through 4: heterosexual single women who had either conceived or adopted. Even though some of these observations may apply equally to the other groups, it is less easy to draw general conclusions regarding them, either because they represent too small a sample, or because they are far too heterogeneous.

The majority of the single women who conceived or

adopted were baby boomers who had been raised in intact families; yet many described their parents' marriages in less than positive terms. Although the fifties marked the high point in this century regarding actual number of traditional families, we know that many of the so-called idyllic marriages of that time were far from blissful.

Many of these women felt that the model of marriage that they had witnessed while growing up had left them wary of repeating a similar pattern. Although their childhood experiences had not deterred them from becoming parents, many felt that these experiences had been a major contributor to their having remained single. Most, nonetheless, said that they would have preferred to have a child with a partner.

Most of these women function well in many areas of their lives, both socially and professionally. Many are well informed, intelligent, and insightful, and a large number have been in therapy at some point in their lives. However, an area in which they had not had the same degree of success was their romantic lives. Many of the women felt that they had not been very good in selecting partners for themselves and had tended to gravitate toward men who were "bad" for them. Others felt that they had problems in maintaining relationships. Although able to establish lasting friendships, many found themselves experiencing some anxiety when they became closely involved in a romantic relationship.

During the course of the interviews, it became apparent that some definite shifts had taken place in their attitudes toward men once they had become mothers. Moreover, two distinctive patterns emerged. The demands of motherhood, particularly having to assume full responsibility for the life of another, led some of them to become more confident in their ability to handle romantic alliances. Becoming mothers had been a maturing process, allowing them to feel more ready to deal with the ambiguities of a romantic relationship.

Becoming mothers had made others now wonder if what they had really wanted all along was a child, and whether they had merely viewed men as a means to that end. Women are often seen as having a stronger sex or maternal drive, and perhaps in these women, the maternal drive was the dominant one.

Because men constituted a much smaller part of this study, it is more difficult to come to any general conclusions concerning them. Single fatherhood is still something of a rarity and is generally viewed as extremely untraditional. Fathers raising their children alone have to contend with such diverse attitudes as being viewed as saintly or as incapable of knowing how to handle children. In order to deal with such stereotypes, these men have to be very determined, perhaps even more determined than single women, in their desire to father their children.

Common denominators among these fathers were the degree of comfort they felt in the nurturing role and their ability to connect with their children emotionally. Many spoke of having wanted to be a parent for almost as long as they could remember. Among the divorced fathers, many had been the more nurturing parent even before the divorce had taken place.

Studies on single fathers have come up with similar findings, concluding that strongly nurturant feelings are not the exclusive domain of women. In one extensive review of the research literature, most fathers were found to be doing a relatively good job in raising their children and to feel very capable of providing for their children's emotional as well as material needs. Some fathers described themselves as being very child-oriented and had been closely involved with their children from the time they were born. Boys were generally found to be doing better than girls who were raised by single fathers. However, some data suggested that girls benefited if they were able to put some emotional distance between themselves and their fathers.[21]

In one study of fathers who had sole custody of children covering a range of ages, no significant differences were found between the fathers' feelings about their children and the nurturing role and the feelings of mothers in comparable circumstances.[22] These findings again suggest that men are just as capable as women of fulfilling the nurturing role. But then, not all women want to be mothers!

None of the above studies included single adoptive fathers. Rather, they were based on men who had previously been married and had custody of their children following the divorce.

Although some of the men who were interviewed here did discuss having difficulties with relationships, this theme was not as pronounced as for the women. Many felt comfortable with their lives and had no particular desire to become involved in a serious romantic relationship. Although some felt that this attitude was a little unusual, the imperative to find a mate was simply not as strong a factor in their lives as it was for some of the women. Because society conveys the message that it is less acceptable for a woman to remain single than it is for a man, women, no doubt, are more indoctrinated in this pattern.

Of the limited research that has been done on single-parent families, much is methodologically flawed because of researcher bias that views anything short of the nuclear family as inevitably deficient.[23] Wallerstein and Blakeslee have suggested that we need a new model for looking at families of divorce. Perhaps we also need a different model for examining single-parent families. Herzog and Sudia state:

> It would be useful to give clearer recognition to the one-parent family as a family form in its own right—not a preferred form, but nevertheless one that exists and functions and represents something other than mere absence of true familiness. We need to take account of its strengths as well as its weaknesses; of the characteristics it shares with two-parent families as well as its differences; of ways in which it copes with its undeniable difficulties; and of ways in which the community supports or undermines its coping capacity.[24]

This is not to say that one cannot have the view that the two-parent family is preferable, rather:

> We should be willing to assert our cultural preference for traditional norms such as marriage and the two-parent home while at the same time accommodating and reaching out to those who have chosen to lead their lives within alternative settings.[25]

For the times, they are a'changin.' One wonders if Bob Dylan knew just how prophetic those words were when he first sang them in the sixties. I recently heard someone say that you cannot stop progress, that sometimes it is good and sometimes it is bad. There is no way we can turn the clock back and return to the values of the fifties, nor would most of us want to. Although we may hold to the belief that two parents are better than one, in one form or another the single-parent family is clearly here to stay. What makes this particular group of single parents different from our usual understanding of the term is that most of them arrived at their decision only after a great deal of soul searching, and that they are highly committed to their children.

It is incumbent on us to have a clearer understanding of how these new family forms work. Perhaps such an understanding will provide insights into how we can deal more effectively with the numerous single-parent families that are not in that circumstance by choice. How successful these men and women are in raising their children and how these new families may ultimately be integrated into the families of tomorrow, time will tell.

Select Directory of Resources

Chapters 1 and 2

Single Mothers By Choice Inc.

200 East 84 Street
New York, NY 10028
212-988-0993

National organization for single mothers and those considering becoming single mothers.

Single Parents Resource Center

141 West 28 Street, Suite 302
New York, NY 10001
212-947-1221

General information and referral service.

Spermbank-Idant Corp.

645 Madison Avenue
New York, NY 10022
212-935-1430

Sperm bank that accepts unmarried women as applicants.

Chapters 3 and 4

Adoptive Families of America

3333 Highway 100 North
Minneapolis, MN 55422
612-535-4829

Information service. Also provides assistance in adoption for individuals and families. Publishes *OURS* magazine for adoptive families.

Committee for Single Adoptive Parents

P.O. Box 15084
Chevy Chase, MD 20815

Information service for prospective and actual single adoptive parents. No telephone number listed.

International Concerns Committee for Children

911 Cyprus Drive
Boulder, CO 80303
303-494-8333

Provides an annual report with updates on foreign adoption.

Latin American Parents' Association
8646 Fifteenth Avenue
Brooklyn, NY 11228
718-236-8689

A parent support group specializing in Latin American adoptions.

Limear
216-653-81239

Brazilian-based organization dealing with hard-to-place children.

New York Council on Adoptable Children
666 Broadway
New York, NY 10012
212-475-0222

Information, preparation, and referral organization with a focus on adopting children through the foster care system.

New York Singles Adopting Children
P.O. Box 752
Forest Hills Station
Forest Hills, NY 1375
212-289-1705
718-229-7240

Provides support and information to single adoptive parents. Publishes a bimonthly newsletter.

North American Council on Adoptable Children

1821 University Avenue
St. Paul, MN 55104
612-644-3036

Coalition of adoptive parents' support and advocacy groups. Committed to meeting the needs of waiting children.

The Adoptive Parents Committee Inc.

210 Fifth Avenue
New York, NY 10021
212-683-9221

A parent support group for adoptive parents or people interested in adoption and their families. Also advocates for improvements in the adoption and foster care systems.

Chapters 7 and 8

Center Kids

The Center
208 West 13 Street
New York, NY 10011
212-620-7310

Support and social group created for and by families headed by lesbians and gay men who are raising children.

Congregation Beth Simhat Torah

57 Bethune Street
New York, NY 10012
212-929-9498

Gay and lesbian synagogue.

Feminist Women's Health Center

580 Fourteenth Street NW
Atlanta, GA 30318
800-282-6013

191 East Broad Street, Suite 203
Athens, GA 30601
404-353-8500

Comprehensive health care service for women, offering a donor insemination program for all women, regardless of race, marital status, or sexual orientation.

Gay and Lesbian Parents' Coalition International

P.O. Box 50360
Washington, DC 20091
202-583-8029

Worldwide advocacy and support group for lesbian and gay parents, their partners, and their children.

Lambda

666 Broadway
New York, NY 10012
212-995-2306

Legal defense and educational organization that advances the rights of gay people. Also maintains a national network of attorneys.

Maranatha

The Riverside Church
Riverside Drive and 122 Street
New York, NY 10027
212-222-5900

Church-associated gay and lesbian group.

Sperm Bank of California

Telegraph Hill Medical Plaza
3007 Telegraph Avenue, Suite 2
Oakland, CA 94609
415-444-2014

1144 Montgomery Drive
Santa Rosa, CA 95405
707-575-8212

Donor insemination program provided for all women, regardless of race, marital status, or sexual orientation.

Notes

Introduction

1. U.S. Bureau of the Census, Household and Family Characteristics: 1991, and previous reports in this series, Current Population Reports, Ser. P-20, no. 458, Washington, DC, 1992.
2. U.S. Bureau of the Census, Household and Family Characteristics: March 1990 and 1989, *Current Population Reports.* Ser. P-20, no. 447, Washington, DC, 1990, p. 10.
3. "By the Decades: The Troubled Course of the Family and Beyond, 1945–1990," *The Family in America, 4*, May, 1990, p. 4.
4. U.S. Bureau of the Census, Studies in Marriage and the Family, *Current Population Reports,* Ser. P-20, no. 447, Washington, DC, December, 1990.
5. *Annual Abstract of Statistics* (London, England: 1992), Her Majesty's Stationery Office, p. 30.
6. The Quid, Edition Robert Laffont et STE des Encyclopedies Quid, 1990.
7. Francine du Plessix Gray, *Soviet Women: Walking the Tightrope* (New York: Doubleday, 1990).
8. Personal communication, Dr. Martin O'Connell, April 8, 1992.
9. Daniel Yankelovitch, *New Rules* (New York: Random House, 1981), p. 96.
10. U.S. Bureau of the Census, U.S. Population Estimates, *Current Population Reports,* Ser. P-25, no. 1045, Washington, DC, January 1990.

11. G. Gurin, J. Veroff, and S. C. Feld, *Americans View Their Mental Health* (New York: Basic Books, 1960).
12. Yankelovitch, p. xiv.
13. Elizabeth Douvan, Richard Kulka, and Joseph Veroff, "Americans Seek Self-Development, Suffer Anxiety from Changing Roles," *ISR Newsletter,* Institute for Social Research, University of Michigan, Winter, 1979.
14. Yankelovitch, p. 96.
15. Ibid., p. 90.
16. Émile Durkheim, *Suicide* (New York: Free Press, 1966). (Originally published in 1897).
17. Robert Merton, *Social Theory and Social Structure* (New York: Free Press, 1968).
18. Yankelovitch, p. 247.
19. Hannah Arendt, *On Revolution* (New York: Viking, 1963).

Chapter 1

1. National Center for Health Statistics, Advance Report of Final Natality Statistics, 1988, *Monthly Vital Statistics Report,* vol. 39, no. 4, suppl., Hyattsville, MD: Public Health Service, 1990, p. 7.
2. National Center for Health Statistics, Advance Report of Final Natality Statistics, 1989, *Monthly Vital Statistics Report,* vol. 40, no. 8, Hyattsville, MD: Public Health Service, December 1990.
3. Linda B. Williams and William F. Pratt, Wanted and Unwanted Childbearing in the United States: 1973–88, *Advance Data from Vital and Health Statistics,* no. 189, Hyattsville, MD: National Center for Health Statistics, 1990.
4. Personal communication, Stephanie Ventura, February 1991.
5. Stephanie Ventura, Trends and Variations in First Births to Older Women, 1970–86, *Vital Health Statistics 21,* Hyattsville, MD: National Center for Health Statistics, 1989, p. 9.
6. Linda B. Williams and William F. Pratt, Wanted and Unwanted Childbearing in the United States, 1973–88, *Advance Data from Vital and Health Statistics,* Hyattsville, MD: National Center for Health Statistics, 1990, p. 5.
7. Carl N. Degler, *At Odds: Women and the Family in America from*

Revolution to the Present (New York: Oxford University Press, 1980), pp. 420–423.

8. *Webster's New Twentieth Century Century Dictionary* (Cleveland: World, 1978), p. 905.

9. Kingsley Davis, The Forms of Illegitimacy, *Social Forces* 18, October 1939, pp. 77–89.

10. Derek Gill, *Illegitimate Sexuality and the Status of Women* (Oxford: Basil Blackwell, 1977).

11. Neil G. Bennett, David E. Bloom, and Patricia H. Craig, The Divergence of Black and White Marriage Partners, *American Journal of Sociology* 95, November 1989, p. 701.

12. Marcia Guttentag and Paul E. Secord, *Too Many Women? The Sex Ratio Question* (Beverly Hills, CA: Sage, 1983).

13. U.S. Bureau of the Census, *Current Population Report Per Marital Status Living Arrangements,* Ser. P-20, no. 445, Washington, DC, 1990, p. 9.

14. Neil G. Bennett and David E. Bloom, Why Fewer American Women Marry, *New York Times,* December 13, 1986, p. 27.

15. Christine Doudna and Fern McBride, Where Are the Men for the Women at the Top? in *Single Life,* Peter Stein (ed.) (New York: St. Martin's Press, 1981).

Chapter 2

1. Sharyne Merritt and Linda Steiner, *And Baby Makes Two* (New York: Franklin Watts, 1984).

2. Carole Klein, *The Single Parent Experience* (New York: Avon Books, 1973).

3. Marilyn Fabe and Norma Wikler, *Up Against the Clock* (New York: Random House, 1979).

4. Linda Lee, *Out of Wedlock* (Boston: Little, Brown, 1982).

5. Naomi Miller, "The Capacity for Intimacy in Single Mothers by Choice" (New York University; Ann Arbor, Mich. University Microfilms International, 1989): 99–100.

6. Mary Twining Rexford, "Single Mothers by Choice: An Exploratory Study" (California School of Professional Psychology; Ann Arbor, Mich.: University Microfilm International, 1976).

7. Lucy Ward, "Innovative Female Identity: Experiential Anteced-

ents of the Capacity for Non-Traditional Childbearing Choices,"
(Boston University School of Education; Ann Arbor, Mich.: University Microfilms International, 1983).

8. Rexford, p. 56.
9. Phima Engelstein, Maxine Antell-Buckley, and Phyllis Urman-
   Klein, "Single Women Who Elect to Bear a Child," in *Psychological Aspects of Pregnancy, Birthing and Bonding,* ed. Barbara L.
   Blum (New York: Human Sciences Press, 1980).
10. Miller, p. 87.
11. Margaret Louise Fox, "Unmarried Adult Mothers: A Study of the
    Parenthood Transition from Late Pregnancy to Two Months Post-
    partum" (Boston University School of Education; Ann Arbor,
    Mich.: University Microfilms International, 1979).
12. Ruth Mechanek, Elizabeth Klein, and Judith Kuppersmith, "Sin-
    gle Mothers by Choice: A Family Alternative," in *Women, Power
    and Treatment,* ed. M. Braude (New York: Haworth Press, 1987).
13. Fox, p. 175.
14. Patricia Morrisroe, "Mommy Only," *New York Magazine,* June 6,
    1983, pp. 22–29.
15. Sheila B. Kamerman and Alfred J. Kahn, *Mothers Alone: Strate-
    gies for a Time of Change* (Dover, MA: Auburn House, 1988).
16. Miller, p. 85.
17. Ibid., p. 84.
18. Erik H. Erikson, *Childhood and Society* (New York: Norton,
    1950), p. 263.
19. Miller, p. 45.
20. Shere Hite, *Women and Love* (New York: Random House, 1987).
21. Therese Benedek, "Parenthood as a Development Phase," *Journal
    of the American Psychoanalytic Association* 7 (1959): 389–417.

Chapter 3

1. Sigmund Freud, "Family Romances," *The Complete Psychological
   Works of Sigmund Freud (London: Hogarth, 1975), pp. 235–241.*
2. Alfred Kadushin, *Child Welfare Services* (New York: Macmillan,
   1980), p. 535.
3. "Adoption," *Encyclopaedia of Social Work,* 18th ed., vol. 1 (Silver
   Spring, MD: National Association of Social Workers, 1987), pp. 67–75.

4. Kadushin, p. 535.

5. Ibid., pp 536–537.

6. "Standards for Adoption Service," Child Welfare League of America (Washington, D.C.: 1989): 9–13.

7. W. D. Mosher and W. F. Pratt, "Fecundity and Infertility in the United States, 1965–88," *Advance Data from Vital and Health Statistics,* no. 192 (Hyattsville, MD: National Center for Health Statistics, 1990).

8. Kadushin, p. 537.

9. Ethel Branham, "One-Parent Adoptions," *Children* 17 (May–June 1970): 103–107; Velma L. Jordan and William F. Little, "Early Comments on Single-Parent Adoptive Homes," *Child Welfare* (November 1966): 103–107.

10. William Feigelman and Arnold Silverman, "Single-Parent Adoption," in *Chosen Children: New Patterns of Adoptive Relations* (New York: Praeger, 1983), pp. 177–178.

11. C. A. Bachrach, P. F. Adams, S. Sambrano, and K. A. London, "Adoption in the 1980's," *Advance Data from Vital and Health Statistics,* no. 181 (Hyattsville, MD: National Center for Health Statistics, 1989).

12. Arnold R. Silverman and William Feigelman, *Adjustment in Interracial Adoptees: An Overview* (New York: Praeger, 1983), p. 188.

13. "Transracial Adoption Update 1978," New York Chapter, National Association of Black Social Workers, New York, 1978.

14. Personal communication, Mary Beth Seader, June 1991.

15. Personal communication, Blanche Gelbor, April 1991.

16. Personal communication, U.S. Senate Judiciary Committee, Washington, DC, May 1991.

17. Hope Marindin (ed.), *the Handbook for Single Adoptive Parents* (Chevy Chase, MD: Committee for Single Adoptive Parents, 1987), pp. 6–7.

18. Ibid.

Chapter 4

1. Joan Shireman and Penny Johnson, "Single Persons as Adoptive Parents," *Social Service Review* 50 (March 1976): 103–116.

2. Sharon Ann Dougherty, "Single Adoptive Mothers and Their Children," *Social Work* 23 (July 1978): 311–314.
3. William Feigelman and Arnold R. Silverman, "Single Parent Adoptions, " *Social Casework* (July 1977): 418–425.
4. William Feigelman and Arnold R. Silverman, *Chosen Children: New Patterns of Adoptive Relations* (New York: Praeger, 1983), p. 192.
5. Joan F. Shireman, "Growing Up Adopted: An Examination of Some Major Issues," Regional Research Institute for Human Services, Portland State University (August 1988).
6. Alfred Kadushin, "Single-Parent Adoptions: An Overview and Some Relevant Research," *Social Service Review* 44 (September 1970): 271.
7. Rita Simon and Howard Altstein, *Transracial Adoption: A Follow-Up* (Lexington, MA: Lexington Books, 1981).
8. Arnold R. Silverman and William Feigelman, "Adjustment in Interracial Adoptees: An Overview," in *The Psychology of Adoption,* ed. David Brodzinsky and Marshall Schecter (New York: Oxford University Press), pp. 187–198.

Chapter 5

1. Lenore J. Weitzman, *The Divorce Revolution* (New York: Free Press, 1985), p. xvii.
2. U.S. Bureau of the Census, "Studies in Marriage and the Family," *Current Population Reports,* ser. P-23, no. 162, Washington, DC, 1989, p. 4.
3. By the Decades: The Troubled Course of the Family 1945–90 . . . and Beyond, *The Family in America* 4, May 1990, p. 2.
4. U.S. Bureau of the Census, Studies in Marriage and the Family, *Current Population Reports,* Ser. P-23, no. 162, Washington, DC, 1989, p. 3.
5. U.S. Bureau of the Census, Marital and Living Arrangements: March 1988, ser. P-20, no. 433, in Joan Anderson, *The Single Mother's Book,* Atlanta: Peachtree Publishers, 1990, p. 2.
6. U.S. Bureau of the Census, Studies in Marriage and the Family, *Current Population Reports,* Ser. P-23, no. 162, Washington, DC, 1989, p. 3.

7. Larry L. Bumpass and James A. Sweet, Children's Experience in Single-Parent Families: Implications of Cohabitation and Marital Transitions, *Family Planning Perspectives* 21, 1989, p. 256.

8. B. F. Wilson, National Center for Health Statistics, Remarriages and Subsequent Divorces: United States, *Vital and Health Statistics,* Ser. 21, no. 45, Public Health Service, Washington, DC, 1989, p. 2.

9. Weitzman, p. 6.

10. Lawrence Friedman, A History of American Law, in Judith Areen, *Cases and Material on Family Law*, 2nd ed. (Westbury, NY: Foundation Press, 1985), pp. 245–246.

11. Michael E. Lamb, ed., *Non-Traditional Families* (Hillsdale, N.J.: Erlbaum, 1982), p. 3.

12. Weitzman, pp. 219–220.

13. Ibid., pp. 15–21.

14. Judith Areen, *1991 Supplement to Cases and Materials on Family Law,* 2nd ed. (Westbury, NY: Foundation Press, 1991), p. 85.

15. Weitzman, 22–23.

16. Lawrence Friedman, "Rights of Passage: Divorce Law in Historical Perspective," as quoted in Areen, 1991, p. 85.

17. Ronald L. Howard, *A Social History of American Family Sociology 1865–1940* (Westport, CT: Greenwood Press, 1981), pp. 13–15.

18. Ibid., p. 16.

19. Suzanne Bianchi and Edith McArthur, U.S. Bureau of the Census, Family Disruption and Economic Hardship: The Short Run Picture for Children, Current Population Reports, ser P-70, no. 23, Washington, DC, January 1991.

20. Weitzman, p. 36.

21. Heather Wishik, Economics of Divorce: An Exploratory Study, in Judith Areen, *1988 Supplement to Cases and Materials on Family Law,* 2nd ed. (Westbury, NY: Foundation Press, 1988), p. 95.

22. Bianchi and McArthur.

23. Betty Friedan, *It Changed My Life* (New York: Random House, 1976), p. 326, as quoted in Weitzman, p. 360.

24. Areen, p. 188.

25. Carol Gilligan, *In a Different Voice* (Cambridge, MA: Harvard University Press, 1982), p. 7.

Chapter 6

1. Judith S. Wallerstein and Sandra Blakeslee, *Second Chances* (New York: Ticknor & Fields, 1989), p. 14.
2. Lenore J. Weitzman, *The Divorce Revolution* (New York: Free Press, 1985), p. 215.
3. Wallerstein and Blakeslee, p. 278.
4. E. Mavis Hetherington and Roger Cox, "Effects of Divorce on Parents and Children," in *Non-Traditional Families,* ed. Michael E. Lamb (Hillsdale, NJ: Erlbaum, 1982), p. 275.
5. Judith S. Wallerstein, Shauna B. Corbin, and Julia M. Lewis, "Children of Divorce: A 10-Year Study," in *Impact of Divorce, Single Parenting, and Stepparenting on Children,* ed. E. Mavis Hetherington and Josephine D. Arasteh (Hillsdale, NJ: Erlbaum, 1988), pp. 197–214.
6. John Guidubaldo, "Differences in Children's Divorce Adjustment across Grade Level and Gender: A Report from the NASP-Kent State Nationwide Project," in *Children of Divorce,* ed. Sharlene A. Wolchik and Paul Karoly (New York: Gardner Press, 1988), p. 187.
7. Jane Elliot, Gay Ochiltree, Martin Richards, Christine Sinclair, and Fiona Tasker, "Divorce and Children: A British Challenge to the Wallerstein View," *Family Law* (August, 1990), pp. 309–310.
8. Hetherington and Cox, pp. 261–262.
9. Robert D. Hess and Kathleen A. Camara, "Post Divorce Family Relationships as Mediating Factors in the Consequences of Divorce for Children," *Journal of Social Issues* 33 (1979): 80–90.
10. Kathleen A. Camara and Gary Resnick, "Interparental Conflict and Cooperation: Factors Moderating Children's Post-Divorce Adjustment," in *Impact of Divorce, Single Parenting, and Stepparenting on Children* ed. E. Mavis Hetherington and Josephine D. Aresteh (Hillsdale, NJ: Erlbaum, 1988), pp. 193–194.
11. Frank F. Furstenberg, Jr., Max N. Term, Heidi Berry Term, and Kathleen Jullan Harris, "The Disappearing American Father? Divorce and the Waning Significance of Biological Parenthood," Department of Sociology, University of Pennsylvania (March 1990).
12. Weitzman, p. 216.
13. Wallerstein and Blakeslee, p. 14.

Chapter 7

1. Roberta Achtenberg, "Preserving and Protecting the Families of Lesbians and Gay Men," *Lesbian Rights Project,* 1370 Mission St., San Francisco, 1986, p. 4.
2. John Boswell, Christianity, Social Tolerance, and Homosexuality, p. 43, cited in Richard C. Friedman, *Male Homosexuality,* New Haven, CT: Yale University Press, 1988.
3. A. C. Kinsey, W. B. Pomeroy, and C. E. Martin, *Sexual Behavior in the Human Male* (Philadelphia: Saunders, 1948).
4. A. C. Kinsey, W. B. Pomeroy, and C. E. Martin, *Sexual Behavior in the Human Female* (Philadelphia: Saunders), 1953.
5. Gordon Rattrey Taylor, Historical and Mythological Aspects of Homosexuality, in *Sexual Inversion,* ed. Judd Marmor (New York: Basic Books, 1965), p. 162.
6. Kenneth Lewes, *The Psychoanalytic Theory of Male Homosexuality* (New York: Simon & Schuster, 1988), p. 13.
7. Judith C. Brown, *Immodest Acts* (New York: Oxford University Press, 1986), p. 6.
8. Richard Isay, *Being Homosexual* (New York: Farrar, Straus, & Giroux, 1989), p. 4.
9. Lewes, p. 29.
10. Sigmund Freud, "Letter to Jones," *Body Politic* (Toronto, Canada, 1977) p. 9.
11. Sigmund Freud, "Letter to an American Mother," in Letter 277 in *The Letters of Sigmund Freud,* selected and edited by Ernst Freud (New York: McGraw-Hill, 1960), pp. 423–424.
12. Lewes, p. 82–85.

Chapter 8

1. Editors of the Harvard Law Review, *Sexual Orientation and the Law* (Cambridge: Harvard University Press, 1990): 120–122.
2. Karen Gail Lewis, "Children of Lesbians: Their Point of View," *Social Work* (May 1980): 198.
3. Editors of the *Harvard Law Review,* pp. 127–129.
4. Ibid., pp. 129–131.
5. Mary E. Hotvedt and Jane Barclay Mandel, "Children of Lesbian

Mothers," in *Homosexuality: Social, Psychological and Biological Issues,* ed. W. Paul, D. Weinrich, J. C. Gonsiorek, and M. E. Hotvedt (Beverly Hills, CA: Sage, 198), pp. 280–282.

6. Richard Green, "Sexual Identity of 37 Children Raised by Homosexual or Transsexual Parents," *American Journal of Psychiatry* 135 (1978): 692–696.

7. Martha Kirkpatrick, Catherine Smith, and Ron Roy, "Lesbian Mothers and Their Children: A Comparative Survey," *American Journal of Orthopsychiatry* 51 (1981): 545–551.

8. Hotvedt and Mandel, p. 283.

9. Karen Gail Lewis, "Children of Lesbians: Their Point of View," *Social Work* (May 1980): 199.

10. Saralie Bisnovich Pennington, "Children of Lesbian Mothers," in *Gay and Lesbian Parents,* ed. Frederick W. Bozett (New York: Praeger, 1987), pp. 63–65.

11. Frederick W. Bozett, "Gay Fathers: Evolution of the Gay-Father Identity," *American Journal of Orthopsychiatry* 51 (July 1981): 554–555.

12. Editors of the *Harvard Law Review,* p. 133.

13. U.S. Congress, Office of Technology Assessment, *Artificial Insemination: Practice in the United States: Summary of a 1987 Survey—Background Paper,* OTA-BP-BA-48 (Washington, D.C.: U.S. Government Printing Office, August 1988): 3.

14. Editors of the *Harvard Law Review,* pp. 142–143.

15. Janet Kornblum, "The Best Interests of the Children? Adoption and Donor Insemination Issues," *Bay Times* (April 1988).

Chapter 9

1. David Popenoe, Beyond the Nuclear Family: A Statistical Portrait of the Changing Family in Sweden, *Journal of Marriage and the Family* 49, February 1987, pp. 173–183.

2. *Population Changes 1990, Part III,* Official Statistics of Sweden, Stockholm, 1991.

3. Steven Bayme, Strengthening the Two-Parent Home, in *Rebuilding the Nest,* ed. David Blankenhorn, Steven Bayme, and Jean Bethke Elshtain, Family Service America, 1990, p. 258.

4. Ibid., p. 178.

5. Ibid., p. 178.
6. Peter Tatchell, *Out in Europe: A Guide to Lesbian and Gay Rights in 30 European Countries*, London, Channel 4 Television, 1990.
7. Anne Marie Tietjen, "The Social Networks and Social Support of Married and Single Mothers in Sweden," Journal of Marriage and the Family (May 1985: 489–500.
8. "Will You Join Me in Civil Unionlock?" *The Economist,* May 2, 1992, p. 59.
9. Lawrence Stone, *Road to Divorce* (Oxford: Oxford University Press, 1990).
10. John Haskey, "One-Parent Families and Their Children in Great Britain: Numbers and Characteristics," Demographic Analysis and Vital Statistics Division, Office of Population and Census Surveys, 1989.
11. Stephen Goodwin, "EC Urged to Enforce Homosexual Rights," *The Independent,* April 21, 1990.
12. John Savage, "Taking Away a Civil Liberty," *Observer* February 10, 1991, p. 49.
13. Mary Browning, "Single Mothers in Gingerbread," *Ginger* (April–May 1990): 8, and "In My Opinion," *Ginger* (June–July 1990): 8.
14. Jean Renvoize, *Going Solo: Single Mothers by Choice* (London: Routledge & Kegan Paul, 1985).
15. Personal communication with Professor Ariel Rosenzvei, Dean of Tel Aviv University Faculty of Law, September 17, 1991.
16. Herb Keinon, "A Damn-Awful Combination of Soviet Emigres," *Jewish Week,* December 20, 1991, p. 25.
17. "Hard, but Not Impossible," *Davar,* July 7, 1988.

Chapter 10

1. *Braschi v. Stahl Associates Co.,* 74 N.Y. 2d 201, 543 N.E.2d 49, 544, N.Y.S. 2d 784 (1989).
2. Katie Monagle, "Court Backs Two-Mom Family," *Ms.,* October 1989, p. 69.
3. Charles A. Waehler, "Personality Characteristics of Never-Married Men." Paper presented at the 99th Annual Convention of the American Psychological Association, San Francisco, August 16, 1991.

4. Janice Ellen Witzel, "Lives of Well-Functioning Never-Married Women: Myths and Realities." Unpublished doctoral dissertation, Northwestern University, 1991.
5. Arnold Modell (Chairman), "The Oedipus Complex: A Re-evaluation." Panel, presented at Annual Meeting of the American Psychoanalytic Association, May 1, 1983. *Journal of the American Psychoanalytic Association* 33 (1985): 201–216.
6. Anna Freud and Dorothy T. Burlingham, "War and Children," in Peter B. Neubauer, "The One-Parent Child and His Oedipal Development," in *The Psychoanalytic Study of the Child* 15 (New York: International Universities Press, 1960): 286–309.
7. Ernest L. Abelin, "The Role of the Father in the Separation-Individuation Process," in *Essays in Honor of Margaret Mahler* ed. J. B. McDevitt and C. F. Settlage (New York: International Universities Press, 1971), pp. 229–252.
8. Ernest L. Abelin, "Some Further Observations and Comments on the Earliest Role of the Father," *The International Journal of Psychoanalysis* 56 (1975): 293–302.
9. Irene Stiver, "Beyond the Oedipus Complex: Mothers and Daughters," *The Stone Center,* No. 26, 1986. Wellesley College, Wellesley, MA.
10. Abelin, "The Role of the Father," 249.
11. David Popenoe, "Fostering the New Familism," in *Perspectives on the New Familism.* An Institute for American Values Working Paper, June 1991. Publication No. WPS, p. 21.
12. Barbara Dafoe Whitehead, "The New Familism," in *Perspectives on The New Familism.* An Institute for American Values Working Paper, June 1991. Publication No. WPS, pp. 1–7.
13. David Popenoe, personal communication, October 21, 1991.
14. Sylvia Ann Hewlett, *A Lesser Life: The Myth of Women's Liberation in America* (New York: Morrow, 1986), p. 184.
15. *The New York Times,* May 25, 1991, p. 11.
16. Frank F. Furstenberg, Jr., Max N. Term, Heidi Berry Term, and Kathleen Jullan Harris, "The Disappearing American Father? Divorce and the Waning Significance of Biological Parenthood," March 1990, Department of Sociology, University of Pennsylvania.
17. Personal communication, David Blankenhorn, October 14, 1991.
18. Urie Bronfenbrenner, "Discovering What Families Do," in David Blankenhorn, Steven Bayme, and Jean Bethke Elshthain (eds.),

Rebuilding the Nest (Milwaukee, WI: Family Service America, 1990).

19. Andrew J. Cherlin, Frank F. Furstenberg, Jr., P. Lindsay Chase-Lansdale, Kathleen E. Kiernan, Philip K. Robins, Donna Ruane Morrison, and Julien I. Teitler, "Longitudinal Studies of Effects of Divorce on Children in Great Britain and the United States," *Science* 252 (June 7, 1991): 1386–1389.

20. Robert S. Weiss, "Growing Up a Little Faster: The Experience of Growing Up in a Single-Parent Household," *Journal of Social Issues* 35 (1975): 97–111.

21. Norma Radin and Graeme Russell, "Increased Father Participation and Child Development Outcomes," in *Fatherhood and Family Policy,* ed., Michael Lamb and Abraham Sagi (Hillsdale, NJ: Erlbaum, 1983) pp. 191–218.

22. Geoffrey L. Groif, *Single Fathers* (Lexington, MA: Lexington Books, 1985).

23. Elaine A. Blechman, "Are Children with One Parent at Psychological Risk? A Methodological Review," *Journal of Marriage and the Family* 44, 1 (February 1982): 179–195.

24. Elizabeth Herzog and Cecilia E. Sudia, "Fatherless Homes," *Children* 15 (1968): 181.

25. Steven Bayme, "Strengthening the Two-Parent Home," in *Rebuilding the Nest,* ed. David Blankenhorn, Steven Bayme, and Jean Bethke Elshtain (Milwaukee, WI: Family Service America, 1990), p. 258.

Index